Managing Quality in the Service Sector

Mike Asher

**KOGAN
PAGE**

YOURS TO HAVE AND TO HOLD

BUT NOT TO COPY

First published in 1996

Kogan Page Limited
120 Pentonville Road
London N1 9JN

British Library Cataloguing in Publication Data

A CIP record for this book is available from the British Library.

ISBN 0 7494 1954 7

Typeset by Northern Phototypesetting Co Ltd, Bolton
Printed in England by Clays Ltd, St Ives plc

Contents

PREFACE

This book is about the improvement of performance in service and administration when there may be no tangible 'product' or output. It is about how those organisations can come to understand what is important to themselves and their customers and how they organise to deliver it. It is about how that message is transmitted through the organisation to the doers, those whose actions ultimately lead to the strategy of the organisation being delivered. It is about giving a mechanism to measure, manage and improve performance in an environment that often seems to militate against such measurement.

The book describes a process for improvement and the steps needed to make that process happen at all levels within the organisation. Various tools and techniques to assist in the process are also given. It is not, however, meant as a 'Royal Road' or prescriptive set of rules that all have to apply. There are many choices – this book highlights these.

It is written in the early chapters to appeal to those who must understand how the strategy they set has to be driven down the organisation into workable parts that can then be made real. Later chapters give techniques to take this and manage the process for improvement. Finally, a case study shows the whole process in action.

Mike Asher
Spring 1996

ACKNOWLEDGEMENTS

Consultants by their nature have a peripatetic lifestyle, moving between family, clients and other consultants. All provide an opportunity for learning and enrichment. These acknowledgements recognise a debt to the many that have contributed indirectly to this book.

Inevitably, the time spent in a major consultancy, PA Consulting Group, and therefore time spent talking over ideas with them has had an impact on learning. Particular thanks go to David Cook, Martin Newman and Kevin Parker. Other people, notably John Macdonald at REL, also contributed.

Probably most time is spent with clients so particular thanks are due to those – Len Horton at British Gas, Paul Waplington at DHL, Dave Procter at British Steel and Bill Snaith at Durham University Business School – who have acted as sounding boards for ideas. Clients after all provide the opportunity to test theory. It would be impossible to thank all by name but most are in here somewhere.

Time spent over a word processor is time spent away from a young family who suffer, mostly in silence, as the work goes on. Anyone who has written will understand that there are difficult times when the words won't come out and you become hard to live with. My thanks go to my wife Dianne and sons Simon and James for living with me whilst this went on.

Finally, all the mistakes are my own. If you find any or don't like the book please tell me; if you do like it, tell others.

INTRODUCTION

The speed of change over the past decade, fuelled as it has been by major changes in software performance and the increasing globalisation of markets creating a world market in many areas, has made many organisations subject their activities to a radical rethink.

This pace of change will only increase as the world effectively becomes a smaller place. The effect of ease of transport combined with the decrease in costs will ensure that this is so.

Underlying these changes have been several key threads:

- *Customers* have realised their power and taken charge. In private sector markets, customers have demanded mass market products that are at the same time customised for them and have demanded to be treated as individuals. In the public sector changes, for example in the National Health Service, have provided choice and traditional customers can easily take their business elsewhere.
- *Competition* has intensified. Competitors have taken advantage of changes in technology to attack niche markets. Public sector organisations have seen competitive tendering lead to competition in refuse collection and many other areas.
- *Technology* – particularly changes in information technology – has made the interchange of data easier and faster. This has led to some slower, more traditional paper-based organisations – particularly in the service sector – having to undertake a radical rethink of their businesses.
- *Change* has become the only constant. The nature of change has itself changed. Lifecycles of products and services have reduced dramatically and organisations need to move faster and faster to keep up.

Organisations created to survive on stability will find it ever harder to survive a world order based upon customers, competition and change itself demanding flexibility.

Changes locally in the European Union have already led to French and German organisations competing by right in the UK and vice versa where previously markets had been closed.

Ideas and principles established over a hundred years ago have shaped the organisational structure, management and performance of most well-established organisations. Organisational ideas stemming from the railways and armed forces – where a command and control system was necessary – have become increasingly out of place when organisations must move fast to survive.

These organisations have concentrated on activity rather than on results, on departmental structures rather than on satisfying customer needs and on introspection rather than understanding the changing marketplace.

Rules, paradigms and structures left over from a very different world still determine how organisations behave. Rules about customers, the market and competitors are often based upon assumptions that no longer hold.

Organisations grow, become introspective and self-serving, and develop a bureaucracy to support activities that have no part to play in customer satisfaction. They simply satisfy the internal needs of the organisation's own structure.

The need to challenge basic assumptions about activities carried out within an organisation – not asking 'can we do it better?' but 'why is it done?' – can lead to dramatic changes.

Increasingly, performance improvement has become a strategic issue for many organisations, and it has changed from a reactive, defensive issue to a proactive, aggressive one.

1

THE EVOLUTION OF QUALITY MANAGEMENT

After centuries when the concepts of quality and quality improvement remained fundamentally unchanged there have been a great many changes since the Second World War.

Starting with very simple *inspection*-based systems where traditionally an organisation would employ people to examine and check the work of others, the basis of this system was that any work below a certain standard would be found before it reached a customer, so documents etc. were proofread for error and when found the errors would be corrected.

The results from this were several. Firstly, the checkers often failed to identify poor quality work and the customers were left with the consequences.

Secondly, this way of producing good quality work – by identifying and segregating poor quality work – is costly, as after all someone is paid to do the checking; inefficient, as it often simply does not work; and wrongheaded in that it has the effect of removing the responsibility for good quality away from those producing the work to those checking it afterwards.

Systems based upon inspection have been around since the Egyptians built the pyramids.

The first change came at the time of the Second World War when technology was becoming more complex and the costs in terms both of people and equipment of relying on inspection-based systems for such things as military aircraft were seen to be unacceptable.

The change was to a system of *quality control* under which product testing and documentation control became the ways to ensure greater process control and reduced failure. Also typical of such systems were the collection of data on performance, feedback of information and the beginnings of self-inspection.

The next major change was away from product quality towards systems quality. Here the organisation sets in place a system for controlling what is done and the system is then audited to ensure that it is adequate in both design and in use. A major part of this change to *quality assurance* involves the use of outside bodies such as BSI, Yarsley and Lloyds to carry out what are called third-party audits to assess the efficiency of the system.

In all of these areas the emphasis is on product quality and manufacturing. Little if any attention has been paid to service industries, service departments or the 'soft' areas of quality such as delivery.

Twenty years ago quality effectively meant product quality and all quality improvement was aimed at product quality improvement. However, when many manufacturing organisations examined the causes of complaints or warranties they found that as few as 20 per cent of these were about the product itself, the remainder were about the administrative and service areas of the organisation. Issues such as delivery, packaging, timeliness and response featured high on the list. Suddenly, organisations that believed that all customers wanted was a good quality product had to change their view and involve all parts of the organisation in satisfying customers' needs.

The changes brought about by the ideas of quality assurance, together with a growing realisation that customers want more than a quality product – they want to deal with a quality organisation – brought first of all service or administration departments into quality improvement and then service organisations themselves followed.

This development towards *total quality management* began in the UK in the early 1980s. Typical of an organisation going through a total quality process would be a clear and unambiguous vision, few departmental barriers, time spent on training, excellent customer relations and the realisation that quality was not just product quality but the quality of the organisation as a whole.

Fundamental to total quality management are the ideas that everyone in the organisation has a customer, internal or external, that improvement comes from understanding and improving business processes and that quality has to be seen to be led from the most senior levels in the organisation.

This focus on processes and therefore on quality improvement via process improvement made it possible for the first time for service and administration areas to take a full part in improvement activities.

Before this it had been difficult for those in service roles to focus on what was done – now they could focus on the process that produced the result rather than the result itself.

2

COMPETING TECHNOLOGIES FOR IMPROVEMENT

There are currently six competing technologies for improvement available. Each of these focuses on processes as a route for improvement.

These technologies are:

- benchmarking;
- total quality management;
- process simplification;
- ISO 9000;
- business process re-engineering;
- competitive tendering/market testing.

Each of them involves processes. The improvement of business processes is now widely seen as the main way any business needs to follow to bring about lasting improvement.

Taking a reasoned decision about the way forward demands an understanding of all of them.

INTRODUCTION TO BENCHMARKING

The definition of benchmarking is 'the process by which internal processes or services are evaluated and later compared with the performance of others'.

Benchmarking is all about identifying gaps in performance and closing these gaps by putting in place best practice, thereby establishing superior performance. It is therefore a form of gap analysis.

Traditional management has focused on internal issues and departmental improvement, firefighting at the expense of longer-term issues. Products, processes, services and standards have often grown unplanned and undesigned.

Benchmarking is a technique that is used to take an independent look at performance by comparing one's own with the performance of others, so setting an agenda for improvement.

Another advantage of benchmarking is that it provides an introduction to the idea of measurement and assists with measurement setting on key business processes. Organisations that have previously been shy of measurement find that, through the introduction of benchmarking, measurement comes naturally.

Reasons for Benchmarking

Robert Camp in his book *Benchmarking – The Search for Industry Best Practices that Lead to Superior Performance* (1989) illustrates the difference in competitive behaviour with and without the practice of benchmarking.

Organisations that do not adapt benchmarking are usually characterised as:

Internally focused, without a clear understanding of their strengths and weaknesses, a reactive approach to competitiveness and a poor knowledge of customers' true requirements. Feeble efforts to innovate.

Organisations that do practise the science of benchmarking can on the other hand be described as:

Proactive, externally focused and close to the markets they operate in. They have access to a limitless pool of ideas, use the market as a starting point for setting their objectives and have a good understanding of customer requirements. They also tackle big problems to achieve major improvements.

Benchmarking therefore needs to be applied for a variety of reasons:

- It is an excellent strategic planning method and as such avoids unrealistic objectives and leads to credible targets.
- It exposes organisations to state-of-the-art practices and, by instigating a continuous learning process, benchmarking can help in the cultivation of a culture of continuous improvement.
- It is a very good vehicle for people education, involvement, empowerment and for optimising their creative potential.

Types of Benchmarking

There are three distinct types of benchmarking that can be applied in any organisation. These can be seen as a progression that an organisation can use to stimulate the improvement process.

Internal Benchmarking

Internal benchmarking is the comparison between functions, departments or a similar organisation as a means of improving performance. The usual aim is to optimise process performance by the removal of errors.

One example of this would be an organisation like the couriers DHL, where many units carry out very similar activities. The organisation has identified key processes and established best working methods. These methods have been transferred to all units.

Another example would be a small company that identified a similar non-competitive company of comparable size and complexity and then carried out a joint benchmarking exercise to allow each to improve. The Grass Roots Group is one company that has begun this process, examining its information technology and accounting processes in this way.

Competitive Benchmarking

This is the cross comparison within one industry sector aimed at establishing gaps in performance between an organisation and its main competitors.

This can be done on a product, service, function, department or company-wide basis. Bayer are actively involved in this type of benchmarking.

Uses of this are widespread in many service industries where organisations regularly 'mystery call' competitors and themselves use an outside agency to report on the response. It is also common in many hotel and retail operations.

Comparative Benchmarking

Comparative benchmarking is the comparison of performance across industry sectors aimed at establishing best practice in all areas of operation.

An example is an organisation that recognises that the issue of export documentation is critical for its success and sets out to establish best business practice for this, regardless of industry.

Organisations going down this route would aim to become world class in the specific areas that they know are critical for themselves and their customers.

An Outline Benchmarking Process

There are two frameworks for benchmarking depending upon the type chosen. These are the *internal* and *external* routes.

The Internal Process

1. Establish the mission and vision.
2. Establish the critical success factors.
3. Establish the key business processes.
4. Decide which processes to benchmark.
5. Identify current performance.
6. Improve the process.
7. Set internal standards.
8. Measure and evaluate.
9. Control and manage the process.

The External Process

1. Establish the mission and vision.
2. Establish the critical success factors.
3. Establish the key business processes.
4. Select a process for benchmarking.
5. Identify partners.
6. Agree a measurement strategy.
7. Compare standards.
8. Identify and understand gaps.
9. Change internal practices.
10. Repeat Step 7.

Lessons to be Learned

There are four generally accepted pitfalls that organisations approaching benchmarking need to be aware of.

The first of these lies in over-ambitious plans at the outset. Benchmarking is unlikely to succeed if an organisation's expectations are unreasonable.

The second lies in the selection of the benchmarking team. Benchmarking is a management function but the team has to include people who have direct experience of the relevant processes.

Choice of external partners is critical to the success of the benchmarking project. Poor choice at the outset, suspicion or ulterior motives will ensure failure.

Lastly, it is too easy to begin benchmarking without proper preparation. There has to be proper planning at the start so that you know what you are comparing and how you are performing before looking outside the organisation.

INTRODUCTION TO TOTAL QUALITY MANAGEMENT

The definition of total quality management is 'the continuous improvement of individuals, groups, departments and organisations focused on meeting customers' requirements'.

Total quality management is about customers - both internal and external, about understanding their needs and then, using a system based on prevention, meeting those needs.

Quality has traditionally been about manufacturing organisations and about product quality. The evolution from inspection-based systems with the reliance on finding bad work, segregating it and if possible carrying out some form of remedial action, to quality control with the emphasis on testing and document control but still containing a large element of inspection, to quality assurance and ISO 9000 with the focus on systems and systems audits had slowly begun to involve non-production operations in quality.

As a consequence of this departments such as finance, marketing, personnel and purchasing had begun to take an active part in quality improvement and the understanding of quality had swung from product quality to company quality and a more holistic approach – total quality – had started.

The emphasis also changed from a system based on finding error – inspection – to a system based on stopping error happening – prevention. This meant a comprehensive understanding of customer needs, organising to meet those needs and planning the actions necessary to keep operations happening right first time.

Since it was possible for non-product departments to be involved in quality it was clearly possible for service organisations to be involved in the same way.

Reasons for Total Quality Management

Organisations had traditionally focused on the quality of the product or service that they had offered. All effort had gone towards getting this right, often at the expense of the wider service offering.

Analysis of complaints in many larger organisations reveals that in most cases customers are to a large extent happy with the basic product or service but experience difficulties with the ancillary services such as delivery, invoicing, packaging and customer contact. These areas had been neglected as management concentrated on the production areas to reduce costs.

As a result, some organisations saw that involving everyone in quality improvement could give them a competitive edge and that total quality could be a way of achieving this.

Fashion had taken many chief executives to Japan to see first hand what had been successfully realised elsewhere and, on their return, they sought to emulate this in their own companies.

There was also a realisation that the figures for quality failure that were so high in manufacturing companies were even higher in the service sector.

Typical quality cost studies in service organisations revealed quality cost figures of between 50 per cent and 60 per cent of the turnover, often the failure cost figure was about 80 per cent of this, or 40 per cent of turnover. These figures offer a major opportunity for improvement in customer service and in cost reduction at the same time.

This combination – of improved customer satisfaction together with reduced cost - was a major driver behind the total quality movement.

The Total Quality Process

Total quality is fundamentally about organisational change with a focus on internal and external customers.

There is a generally recognised four-step process involved with the introduction.

Step 1: Establish the Need to Change

Typically, this involves understanding the cost of quality, carrying out a customer perception survey, internal interviews and in some cases an analysis of supplier perceptions.

This stage forms a vital precursor to a successful total quality process and is necessary for several reasons

Firstly, it convinces an organisation that change is needed. An organisation has grown to be the way that it is – why change it? A picture of the current state of the organisation helps persuade people to change.

Secondly, once the change has begun there is always the temptation to settle for short-term gains. A good reason to begin the process is a good reason to keep going – after all, things are not that different yet!

The next reason is to establish a measure, a benchmark to where we are starting from so that progress can be measured and monitored. Total quality is not about feeling better, it is about enhanced business performance.

Improvement is about priority setting and is as much about deciding what not to do as about deciding what to do. A full understanding of the start point allows priorities to be set and effective planning to take place.

By finding out in detail the starting point you are also beginning to create dissatisfaction with the current state of affairs. This makes it more likely that change will happen.

Step 2: Gaining and Sustaining Commitment

The second stage is to develop and demonstrate senior management leadership of the change process. Total quality is a management-led process and a major part of this second stage is planning how to demonstrate this commitment on two levels.

As an executive, there is a need to lead the process to encourage others to follow and to prove to them that you mean what you say. This can be done in many ways – leading an improvement project, taking on ownership of a business process, acting on a particular internal customer interface and many others. What is vital is that it is done.

At a more personal level it is important to demonstrate a change in behaviour to reinforce the total quality message. This can be one of the most powerful ways of showing others that things are going to be different in the future.

The third element of this stage is the development of a quality vision. This statement of values and beliefs can be an important way of building on the dissatisfaction created during the first stage and focusing people on how they can contribute to change in the future. By debating the role of managers in achieving the vision it is possible to harness their commitment to the change rather than their opposition to it.

Another vital element of this stage is the beginnings of a quality improvement plan. By planning and monitoring quality improvement at the most senior level a strong message can be sent that this is as important as other items monitored at the same level. Quality improvement plans also provide a valuable link into continuous improvement. This moves the organisation away from an 'I've done my bit' approach of single projects towards a structure of continuously planned sequential improvements.

Step 3: Implementation

The implementation stage typically includes education in the principles of total quality, building on the values contained in the vision to ensure that everyone in the organisation shares the same values and beliefs. By doing this it is possible to focus all employees towards the customer.

This is complemented by training in the tools and techniques of quality improvement, so giving people in the improvement process the means to harness the desire to change and make it real. It is the correct balance of 'hearts and minds' and improvement tools that contributes to the success of the process.

Also at this stage would be the setting up of improvement activities based upon the quality improvement plan. These are management-initiated activities focused on bringing about changes to the problems diagnosed during the first stage.

Step 4: Review

Typically, 24 months into the process it is beneficial to go back and carry out Step 1 again, so demonstrating the improvements made.

As well as providing measures to prove success this allows a possible refocus of the process and again shows the way forward into continuous improvement.

The Lessons to be Learned

Careful planning is essential at the early stages of the process to ensure success. Many organisations will attempt a 'kick and rush' approach and this will almost certainly fail. Any approach that involves everyone in an organisation will be long term and complex.

It can be tempting at the beginning of a total quality process to build up expectations that cannot be met resulting in disappointment and failure. The lesson here is the importance of emphasising the long-term nature of total quality and the fact that results are worth waiting for. In this context, total quality is not a quick fix.

During the process it may become apparent that the particular focus being used is not being successful. If this happens be prepared to change course and use another focus for improvement.

To succeed the process needs early successes to encourage others to become involved and these successes need recognition to reinforce the message.

The Advantages of Total Quality

By involving everyone in the organisation, total quality demonstrates that quality is a company-wide issue and that they each have a part to play in quality improvement. This moves quality away from the ghetto of product or process quality towards company quality.

By its nature, total quality creates the environment to encourage individuals to take responsibility for quality improvement in their own jobs. This in turn encourages all to take part.

In contrast to many improvement methodologies, total quality is a management-led process. This allows improvement to be taken at a pace that is acceptable to the whole company.

Whilst ISO 9000 is a system, a set of rules for quality competence, total quality is a philosophy, a way of approaching quality throughout the organisation.

Because of the above advantages, total quality is very visible through the whole organisation and its effects can be seen everywhere.

The Disadvantages of Total Quality

All long-term processes take time to show the benefits, and total quality is no exception. Anyone expecting short-term benefits will be disappointed.

Management-driven processes require sustained levels of management commitment to keep them going and show results. This is time that could be used elsewhere and it is important to recognise the time involvement at the start of the process.

Training and education also take time. The major cost of any total quality process is not consultancy time or materials, it is the internal cost of people being trained and working on teams. Estimates vary, but an average of two days per person in the first year is realistic.

If techniques such as departmental purpose review are used to explore the internal customer interfaces, there can be a temptation to become bogged down in too many details, so obscuring the total picture. This must be avoided.

INTRODUCTION TO PROCESS SIMPLIFICATION

Process simplification is 'a structured approach to continually improve processes'.

Reasons for Process Simplification

The rationale behind process simplification is that quite often processes have grown unplanned and that in many service organisations it can be difficult to see what is done as part of an overall process. Two consequences of this are that tasks are often added but seldom removed and that tasks often move with the people responsible for carrying them out rather than being carried out in the most efficient and effective place.

Process simplification is seen as a way of cutting out the non-value added work in processes and as far as possible ensuring that tasks are carried out in the right place. Both of these lead to smaller, more effective processes that have reduced likelihood of error and therefore fewer failure costs.

The end result is therefore a faster process with reduced error. This in turn gives a reduction in waste and rework and consequently a reduction in the overall cost of the process.

An Outline Process

Process simplification is about understanding how a process works then, by identifying gaps, dead ends, duplications and redundant steps, seeking to improve the process incrementally.

The process involved is very simple.

1. Identify the process to be studied.
2. Identify the study team.
3. Construct an outline flowchart of the process.
4. Draw the detail flowchart of the process.
5. Using the flowchart, identify gaps, dead ends etc.
6. Plan to remove these.
7. Document the new process.
8. Disband the team.

This approach fits well with the quality systems methodology and helps people to understand jobs and processes better.

Advantages of Process Simplification

Process simplification makes the idea of small, incremental changes to process performance acceptable. Things do not have to change dramatically as they do with re-engineering. They can improve by, say, 10 per cent year on year. This fits in well with the ideas behind continuous improvement and total quality.

The incremental size of the changes makes them less threatening to those carrying out the change and therefore more acceptable.

Process simplification involves those close to the process with the changes, therefore making them more likely to be accepted and implemented. The participation of the team in the change is an integral part of process simplification.

Since simplification is at heart a form of gap analysis, measuring current performance as a prelude to changing the processes and then measuring the new state emphasises the role of management by fact and the need to have accurate metrics of performance.

Disadvantages of Process Simplification

As a downside of the above process simplification can be slow and time consuming. The incremental effect of a 10 per cent year-on-year improvement will be great but patience is needed to bring it about and for some organisations that time may not be there.

Process simplification may in fact inhibit major improvements. Why bother with major change when it can be done slowly? Some authors in fact recommend the approach as far more lasting than major change programmes but there can be a danger that simplification can become an end rather than a means.

Lessons to be Learned

There are now many organisations with experience of the simplification process and the lessons to be learned are now clear:

- Don't get bogged down in clever tools and techniques – simplification is a simple process. Don't try to be clever with methodologies that aren't appropriate for what you are trying to achieve.
- Most important processes cross functional boundaries yet people are more comfortable managing and setting improvement targets on tasks within functions or departments. For process simplification to work the functional boundaries between parts of the process must be challenged and where appropriate broken down.
- Very simple tools such as flowcharting and process analysis can pay dividends. It is necessary to train people to use them and then let them use them!
- Use of the correct tools will prevent people seeking to cut corners to get their way in the new process. The use of these tools should not be underestimated.
- All processes that add value in some way serve the customer. It is easy to become introspective and design a perfect process which omits to take customer needs into account. Don't forget the customer!

INTRODUCTION TO BS EN ISO 9000

BS EN ISO 9000 (ISO 9000) is 'a method for guaranteeing consistency of approach through the use of written procedures, systems audits and review'. In other words, it is a systems standard and documents what you do, not what you produce.

There is confusion in that customers see a supplier with ISO 9000 and often assume that this relates to the quality of product or service supplied. It does not – it relates to the documented quality management system operated by the supplier.

Reasons for ISO 9000

Perhaps the major reason that many organisations have followed the ISO 9000 route is customer pressure. Customers find it easy to control their suppliers by demanding ISO accreditation, with the threat that they will cease to be suppliers if they do not comply.

A more positive reason is the realisation that poor quality costs money in the form of waste and rework and that by standardising and documenting what is done money can be saved. A recent Department of Trade and Industry survey estimated that poor quality costs industry between 15 and 30 per cent of turnover and that a good quality management system can save 10 per cent of this figure.

Good written procedures can constitute a significant training method leading to the elimination of error by instructing people in good practices.

A fourth reason is that as organisations grow it becomes more difficult to provide a uniform, consistent approach without written instructions. ISO 9000 provides those instructions.

The ISO 9000 Process

The process for introducing ISO 9000 is deceptively simple and, perhaps for this reason, seldom followed properly.

1. Say what you do. In other words, describe existing methods of operation, elaboration or change.
2. Flowchart the process that you have described taking care to include all elements that may impact on the quality of the outcome.
3. Carry out the process as you have described it in the written procedure.
4. Prove that you are doing it by providing evidence that procedures are being followed. This is usually done by forms or documents.
5. Improve it. ISO accreditation is not an end in itself; there is often scope for improvement in procedures once they are written and consistently followed.

Lessons to be Learned

For maximum effect, people need early involvement in the construction of their own procedures otherwise the procedure will not reflect current practice and will not be followed.

The second lesson is that procedure writing is a critical phase and care at the beginning can help prevent more effort being needed later.

There is a temptation to add rules and documents to existing practice. Bearing in mind that things worked before ISO 9000 each addition should be questioned and justified, otherwise a paper-heavy system may result.

Commitment from the top needs to be demonstrated to convince people to operate the system. It's the managing director's system and it needs to be seen as such. Another approach to this is that 'negative commitment' is disastrous – bucking the system sends a very powerful message but the wrong one.

Advantages of ISO 9000

Without written procedures consistency can be impossible and the ability to pass jobs from one individual to another becomes undermined. ISO encourages consistency.

The cycle of audit – corrective action – management review seen in ISO 9000 gives a mechanism for pointing out shortfalls in the system and encouraging ideas for improvement. In other words, the system is not there to stop change, it can be used to encourage it.

When a new employee joins a department or a manager takes over a new role the written procedures provide an invaluable training aid, setting out in detail the job requirements.

By having laid down procedures and standards an organisation can justifiably claim that in the event of problems it had taken due care and had not been negligent in its operations.

Disadvantages of ISO 9000

The operation of ISO 9000 can be bureaucratic and ISO 9000 often encourages 'closet bureaucrats' to invent more work for others.

Written procedures can become paper-heavy and a nightmare to manage, although recent PC-based document management systems have eased this problem.

By its nature, apart from procedure writing, few employees will be actively involved with the ISO 9000 system. The system can seem remote from them and have little to do with their normal jobs. This impacts on their adherence to the system.

As part of the ISO 9000 system, there has to be a nominated representative with responsibility for the system as a whole. Unless care is shown this can have the adverse impact of taking responsibility for quality away from those carrying out the tasks and placing this with the management representative, so removing part of their responsibilities.

Finally, ISO 9000 is a system for managing quality not an approach to quality. It does not seek to question and improve what happens. It is above all about consistency, not improvement.

INTRODUCTION TO BUSINESS PROCESS RE-ENGINEERING

The definition given by Michael Hammer in his book *Re-engineering The Corporation* (1993) is 'to fundamentally change the way work is performed in order to achieve radical performance improvements in quality, speed and cost'.

At the heart of re-engineering is the idea of discontinuous thinking, of recognising and breaking away from the outdated rules and fundamental assumptions that underlie operations.

The key word in the definition is 'fundamental' - re-engineering is not about incremental change, it is about massive change, possibly affecting the whole structure of an organisation.

Business process re-engineering is a technique that focuses on the mission of an organisation and asks what processes are critical for survival and success. It then subjects those processes to fundamental and far-reaching review. It is therefore not for the faint-hearted.

Reasons for Business Process Re-engineering

Compared with both benchmarking and market testing, re-engineering is the most radical of the approaches. To want to undertake this, to be brave enough to undergo so searching a reappraisal, there must be real need. The underlying reasons therefore for re-engineering are:

- *Survival.* An organisation facing disaster does not have time to tinker at the edges – it has to act or die. Finding a way that is marginally better is not enough. One organisation had a large volume of very profitable business with a customer who traditionally accepted a turnround time of 48 hours. Confronted with a demand for a 12-hour turnround the only option was to reinvent the process completely or lose the business, which would have meant oblivion.
- *The prospect of creating and owning a new market leading to untold riches.* An example here is Direct Line which invented the telephone insurance market and is now doing the same in other areas. The first into a market takes all.
- *Being the best.* Being number one has many advantages for staff, customers and shareholders. The ability to be the best can help you to stay the best, enjoying margins which are the envy of competitors. Coca-Cola is an example in this category.

Re-engineering came about from a realisation that it is not good enough simply to rearrange the deck chairs on the *Titanic* when what was needed was a way of surviving.

It is therefore an all or nothing approach that can produce dramatic changes in performance, not 10 per cent or 15 per cent but in the order of 85 per cent – massive differences.

Any approach that can achieve this has to be thought about and taken seriously or not at all.

An Outline of the Re-engineering Process

The early stages of the re-engineering process are very similar to the process for benchmarking:

1. Establish the mission and vision.
2. Establish the critical success factors.
3. Establish the key business processes.
4. Decide which processes to re-engineer.
5. Evaluate current performance.
6. Analyse why this is so.
7. Starting with a clean sheet, reinvent the process.
8. Compare the two processes.
9. Plan to implement the change.

Lessons to be Learned

Organisations that have undertaken business process re-engineering successfully report very similar experiences.

- Implementing business process re-engineering takes strong leadership and demands substantial time, input and real commitment from the very top of the organisation. The chief executive of one health authority that went through a re-engineering process calculated that it took 70 per cent of his personal time over a six-month period.
- There is a need to know and measure current performance levels so that a baseline can be set. An advantage of this is that problem areas will be identified at the outset of re-engineering. The argument 'we don't need to know how we are doing, we just know it's not good enough' is not a good one, you may end up upsetting a lot of people and have a process that is no better than before.
- Knowledge of mission, success factors and key processes is vital and this can only be developed by the very top of an organisation. Keeping the process going needs a top-level steering group to manage the work. Re-engineering is a strategy-driven process and without that knowledge it would be easy to spend time re-engineering the wrong processes.
- Early involvement of all employees via working teams is necessary to bring about the changes involved. Re-engineering is hard enough anyway so the sooner people can be involved the better. By getting participation in this way some ownership of the changes can be built up.
- Making certain that staff motivation is maintained throughout the process is perhaps the most difficult area. Telling a turkey Christmas is coming is not particularly motivational and most people, rightly, associate re-engineering with job losses.
- Don't be deterred by the difficulty once you have started. Re-engineering is best done in a short sharp blast with no excuses for failure accepted. It can be too easy to listen to other people when you should simply be getting on with it, however unpopular it may be.

INTRODUCTION TO COMPULSORY COMPETITIVE TENDERING/MARKET TESTING

The definition of market testing is 'the process by which in-house functions are exposed to competition'.

Market testing is all about identifying non-core activities and then carrying out a critical evaluation of their effectiveness, thereby giving reduced costs, enhanced productivity and improved quality and leading to improved value for money.

Organisations have grown to satisfy their own needs rather than those of their customers. Departments and structures have appeared that are often remote from satisfying external customer needs and sometimes appear to generate internal customer needs which they can then satisfy.

Market testing is a technique that is used to examine what is done and look for alternative methods of producing the results so giving the organisation better value.

A major advantage of market testing is that it allows an organisation to focus on its core activities, thereby freeing management from managing non-core activities so allowing them to focus on those activities of most value to the organisation.

Reasons for Market Testing

Organisations have grown in response to internal needs – setting up a travel department, hiring a fleet of drivers and vehicle maintenance, having an in-house design team, developing their own publishing house and in many other ways.

None of these areas has a direct impact on the external customer yet they use management time and other costs to keep them going.

In a drive to reduce costs and improve value for money, organisations in the private sector have been keen to reduce overhead costs since the mid-1980s. This has now spread to looking critically at non-overhead areas and to the public sector.

The background to this was the White Paper *Competing for Quality, Buying Better Public Services* published in November 1991.

Between 1991 and 1993, £1.1 billion was market tested giving average savings of 22 per cent. It is worth noting that in-house bid teams won 68 per cent of the tenders that they submitted. Between 1993 and 1994 a further £830 million was tested.

An Outline Process for Market Testing

There are well-established processes for both the internal and tendering parts of market testing.

The Internal Process

1. Appoint a steering group and project manager.
2. Identify and 'ring fence' the current service.
3. Cost the current service.
4. Establish the user requirement.
5. Review potential external suppliers.
6. Develop a detailed specification

The Tender Process

1. Advertise the service to be tendered for.
2. Carry out pre-qualification of tenderers.
3. Invitation to tender.
4. Briefing of potential suppliers.
5. Submission of tenders.
6. Evaluation of quotations.

This is followed by the award of the contract and the monitoring of supplier performance.

Lessons to be Learned

Experience with the market testing process has shown there to be both positive and negative aspects to it. These can be described as follows.

The Advantages

▪ It forces the in-house team to take a hard look at what they do, questioning the value of established practices.
▪ There is a potential reduction of in-house costs as a direct result.
▪ Quality improvements can arise as a result of a better understanding of customer needs.
▪ The review of customer/user needs can reveal both gaps and duplications in performance.
▪ The range of non-core activities is often reduced: 'Why do we do this anyway?'
▪ The process can of itself make service functions more customer aware.
▪ Having a more accurate costing of internal services makes users more aware of costs, leading to more prudent use.
▪ Clarification of boundaries can make responsibilities clearer between internal customers and suppliers.

These advantages need to be weighed against some potential disadvantages.

The Disadvantages

▪ If the contract is awarded externally there will be a discontinuity of service.
▪ There are obvious adverse impacts on staff morale with the increased uncertainty.
▪ The costs of managing external providers must be included in the total cost.
▪ It could be a time-consuming and expensive way of finding out that the in-house service provided excellent value for money.
▪ Generally, the smaller the unit the more difficult it is to apply.

3

AN INTEGRATED FRAMEWORK FOR IMPROVEMENT

Presented as they have been as discrete techniques or methodologies it may seem that an organisation must choose which way to go and then slavishly follow that route.

This is far from the case. With planning it is possible to combine the various methodologies across an organisation and for different parts of organisations to select the most appropriate route for themselves at any time. Provided that the way forward is thought about and planned it is possible to move from one to another for maximum benefit.

The schematic of an integrated improvement framework shown in Figure 3.1 shows how this is possible. For example, having agreed the mission and vision and carried out an organisational diagnosis, it is possible to decide to go down the route of identifying critical success factors and key processes. This may lead to process simplification, benchmarking or re-engineering. The success can then be measured for all to see.

Alternatively, following the diagnosis it may be more appropriate to go directly for ISO 9000 and then follow the process simplification route. Again the savings in process steps can be identified and measured.

Another approach would be to use the idea of internal customers to help people to identify the quality needs in their jobs and to focus on improvement. The improvements in performance for internal customers can be measured and displayed for all to see.

Use of the cost of quality as a driver for improvement could lead to improvement teams aimed at reducing the cost of failure. Cost of quality provides a natural measure allowing people to identify work that adds no value and then work to reduce it.

The common feature of all of these approaches is a managed measured process. The cycle of diagnosis, visioning, action and review as shown in Figure 3.2 forms the basis of permanent improvement. At the end of each cycle the improvement is measured and a decision is taken – do we continue on the same route or do we switch to another method of driving the improvement process?

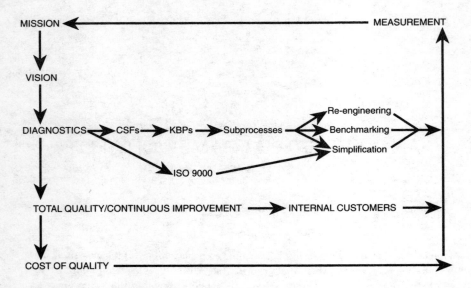

Figure 3.1 *An integrated framework for quality improvement.*

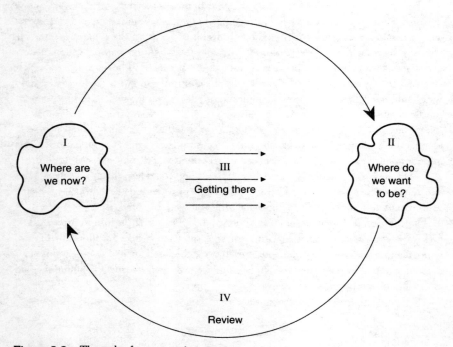

Figure 3.2 *The cycle of permanent improvement.*

Planning improvement in this way has several advantages. Firstly, we all realise in practice that without a continual stimulus the driving force of improvement soon fades and the pressure to keep going drops off. By revisiting this every 18 months the pressure can be kept on and a different focus can bring about renewed efforts.

Secondly, many organisations have in the past been guilty of a 'flavour of the month' approach to management with one fad following another. By describing at the outset how all the different approaches fit under one improvement umbrella the danger of people waiting to 'sit it out' can be removed. We are moving from flavour of the month towards consistency – even if the flavour is now Neapolitan!

Finally, an approach of this nature can after a while revert to the initial approach and repeat the cycle, looking for more improvements in cost of quality, processes or internal customer relationships. In this way permanent improvement can become a way of life.

RESPONSIBILITY FOR PROCESSES

Whether benchmarking, simplifying, ISO 9000 or re-engineering, the mechanism for improvement is processes rather than departments. In other words, there is a move away from traditional management and organisation structures towards management of processes.

There are many implications of this, not least the fact that processes span departments and therefore cross departmental walls. Processes are seen as horizontal whereas departments are vertical structures. It is therefore necessary to appoint individuals to hold responsibility for defining and managing each process.

THE PROCESS OWNER

A process owner is the single named individual responsible for defining and improving the process in its entirety. In the execution of this responsibility, the process owner will need to oversee:

- the definition of the process;
- the continuing effectiveness and efficiency of the process;
- the definition and measurement of process outcome and performance standards;
- the development and maintenance of internal customer/supplier relationships;
- the documentation of the critical activities in the process;
- the creation of an environment for teamwork, open discussion and active participation of all people involved in the process;
- the identification and implementation of process improvements.

This demands certain personal skills and it is important for a process owner:

- to be a role model in teamwork;

■ to have the interpersonal skills, influence and commitment necessary for the purpose;

■ to have the ability to generate enthusiasm and active involvement from all.

With this in mind, process owners should be selected from the part of the organisation most closely involved with the process and should come from as far down the chain of command as feasible. This responsibility for process ownership must be compatible with other organisational responsibilities.

As with other aspects of management, the concept of process ownership is a cascading responsibility. Hence, the chief executive is the owner of the major processes but ownership of sub-processes will be delegated in such a way that ensures that individuals concerned can be brought together to define, measure and improve the process under the team leadership of one individual.

PRACTICAL PROBLEMS IN NEGOTIATING PROCESS OWNERSHIP

The majority of problems encountered when identifying process owners and their roles relate to the interdepartmental interfaces involved.

Most significant processes involve more than one department or function and in most cases the roles and responsibilities relating to the process are less than clearly defined.

This leads to problems, the most frequent of which are:

■ fear by individuals of losing power or authority;

■ interdepartmental rivalry;

■ the assumption that all staff working in the function must report to the process owner;

■ prejudice or belief that one profession considers itself superior to others, and therefore assumes seniority;

■ imbalance of delegation of responsibility and authority;

■ abdication of all responsibility in favour of process owners;

■ the process documentation does not reflect the real process.

Most of these problems are interpersonal problems that indicate that people are talking about process ownership but not practising it.

Problems of this nature can be avoided by ensuring that the balance between the *process* and *people* aspects develop in a balanced and coordinated way.

4

TURNING A MISSION INTO AN AGENDA FOR ACTION

THE MISSION STATEMENT

Successful change processes often begin with a refocusing of the organisation in terms of *mission*. A mission in this sense is a statement of the business that you are in.

The purpose of developing a *mission statement* at the start of an improvement process is to advertise that the intention to change is there. Organisations that use the mission to make the change happen recognise that is a powerful motivational tool.

Viewed in that way a mission statement has several key uses:

- it is a reason for changing, for being different;
- it is a reason for keeping going when the going gets tough;
- it is an ever present standard against which to judge action;
- it can be used to set priorities for improvement;
- it can be used by successive levels of managers to discuss roles and responsibilities;
- it makes change more likely by highlighting the gap between the present and the future desired state.

If a mission statement is worth having, it is worth using to drive the improvement process and to demonstrate that the whole executive team is committed to it.

Mission statements can be used to identify an improvement route, identify top executives with the change process and cement the team together (Asher, 1991; Hardaker and Ward, 1987).

In other words, the mission statement is translated into a programme of action. It is tested to ensure that it is not simply a form of words but a call for a real change.

The first stage is therefore to develop a clear understanding of the team's mission.

If the organisation's mission statement is wrong then everything that follows it is also wrong. A mission is not a collection of individual job descriptions. It defines the boundaries of a business and its customers, and it says what will be done.

DEFINITION OF CRITICAL SUCCESS FACTORS

With the mission in place and agreed the second stage is to identify the *critical success factors (CSFs)* – these are the factors that must be achieved to achieve the mission. Each CSF must be necessary; together they must be sufficient to achieve the mission.

Critical success factors are the limited number of areas in which satisfactory results will ensure successful competitive performance for the individual, department or organisation. The CSFs are the few key areas where 'things must go right' for the organisation to flourish. They must be meaningful to individuals and be capable of being affected by their behaviour.

They are what the executive team together must achieve to accomplish the mission. This rule is vital. The list of CSFs must reflect the absolute minimum of aims that have to be achieved for the team to accomplish the mission.

In addition, each CSF must be devoted to a single issue – the word 'and' cannot be used.

The list should be a mixture of tactical and strategic factors. If all the factors are strategic the business might founder whilst the team concentrates on the blue skies ahead. Equally, if all the factors are tactical, the business could fail due to taking a too short-term view.

The maximum number of CSFs is eight. Few teams can cope with more than this. Problems agreeing the CSFs usually arise from an incorrect or insufficiently focused mission statement.

An example of a large research and technology organisation recently privatised reveals a list of five CSFs:

1. Excellent customer satisfaction.
2. Skilled staff.
3. Technical excellence.
4. Fast reaction time.
5. Excellent suppliers.

The route to derive the list of CSFs is first of all to brainstorm with the team a list of 50-plus items and then to debate the list down until there are only seven or eight items left. These items are then the absolute *must haves* of the business. Consensus on these items is absolutely vital. There must be total agreement – not voting – on the list.

The 'necessary and sufficient' rule can be used to test items to ensure that they need to be on the list.

In a live situation it can take more than half a day to arrive at the last seven CSFs. This list is vital and forms the basis for the next stage.

DEFINITION OF KEY BUSINESS PROCESSES

The third stage is to identify what has to be done so that an organisation can meet its critical success factors. We know what we 'must have' in place to achieve the mission – what business processes must we carry out to achieve this? These processes deliver value to the customer and are critical to the organisation's success.

A *key business process* (*KBP*) is a set of linked activities that respond to a need external to the organisation. As such therefore:

▪ they must be felt or valued by the customer or stakeholder;
▪ they must create an opportunity for differentiation or competitive edge;
▪ they are indifferent to organisation structure;
▪ they are critical to the organisation's success;
▪ they are generally cross functional in scope;
▪ they focus on delivering a result, not monitoring other processes.

These key business processes will be specific and unique to the organisation. Most organisations have a small number of KBPs, generally no more than four or five. The KBPs will together deliver the critical success factors, the 'must haves' of the organisation.

The processes we are discussing are high-level processes which will later break down into sub-processes for management purposes. A few examples show typical processes in different industrial sectors.

In the automobile industry there are normally four KBPs that together deliver the mission:

1. Developing new products.
2. Managing customers and sales.
3. Manufacturing and assembling products.
4. Planning and managing materials.

Similarly, in the pharmaceutical industry the four KBPs are:

1. Managing the regulator.
2. Developing new products.
3. Planning and managing patent protection.
4. Managing product supply and distribution.

In a consultancy organisation the list of KBPs might be:

1. Retaining and developing people.
2. Delivering assignments.
3. Marketing and selling services.

Processes describe what is actually done in the business – they are not bland wish lists. Business processes are the 'verb–nouns' of a business, 'recruiting staff' or 'billing customers', not personnel or invoicing which are names of departments and relate to organisational structure.

As with the CSFs relating to the mission, each KBP must be necessary and the totality of the processes must be sufficient to achieve the list of 'must haves'.

Several other rules relate to the list of key business processes:

▪ Every process should have an owner.
▪ The owner should be a member of the executive team.
▪ No person should own more than three processes.

The route to derive the list of key business processes is first of all to brainstorm with the team a list of 30-plus processes and then to debate the list down until there are approximately 15. These processes are then placed on a matrix against the critical success factors. For each CSF the team asks: 'Which processes need to be performed well to achieve this?'

The aim of this stage is to identify the key business processes. This is done for each process on the list. A total is then made of how many CSFs each of the processes influences.

This is where the mission statement and process improvement fit together. The quality or performance of each process can be measured:

■ Is it being done?
■ By whom?
■ How often?
■ How well?

Now suppose that a complete list of key business processes exists, each of which has an owner. The list is exclusive, since a process must be important to be there, but it still needs ranking to identify the most critical processes, those whose performance or quality will have the greatest impact upon the mission.

The penultimate stage, then, is to rank the processes according to their contribution. Place the processes and CSFs in random order on a matrix and ask the question: 'Which KBP must be performed especially well for us to be confident of achieving this CSF?' The objective is to single out the processes that have a primary impact on this particular CSF. What we are identifying are the essential processes.

When this is performed for the first CSF the question is asked: 'If all these activities are performed well, will the team achieve the CSF?' If the answer is 'no' then the list of processes is incomplete.

This is done in turn for each critical success factor, being careful to apply the necessary and sufficient test before moving on to the next factor.

The final stage is to judge, subjectively if necessary, how well each process is carried out on a scale of A–E (A is excellent, E is informal). An example using the research and technology organisation is shown in Figure 4.1.

Critical Success Factors

	Business Processes	Excellent Customer Satisfaction	Skilled Staff	Technical Excellence	Fast Reaction Time	Excellent Suppliers			Count	Quality
P1	Measure customer satisfaction	✓			✓				2	D
P2	Define product requirements	✓	✓	✓	✓	✓			5	D
P3	Define skill needs	✓	✓	✓					3	D
P4	Train employees technically	✓	✓	✓					3	A
P5	Monitor product performance	✓	✓	✓					4	C
P6	Monitor competitor activity	✓		✓					2	D
P7	Manage the vendor base				✓	✓			2	E
P8	Control projects	✓	✓		✓	✓			4	D
P9	Report progress to customers	✓	✓						2	C
P10	Identify future resource needs	✓	✓	✓	✓	✓			5	D
P11	Identify future customer needs	✓	✓		✓				3	D
P12	Train employees in customer relations	✓	✓		✓				3	D

Figure 4.1 *Matrix for ranking processes.*

The quality of each process is then plotted horizontally and the number of CSFs the process affects is plotted vertically. The team then divides the graph into zones to create groups of processes. Zone 1 contains the most critical processes. This is shown in Figure 4.2.

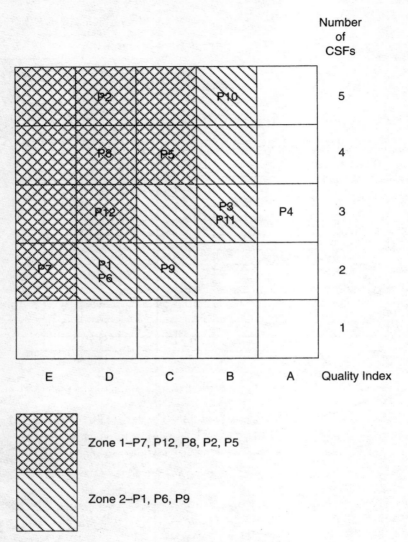

Figure 4.2 *The quality grid.*

At the end of this process there is a list of the most critical processes that must then be improved.

Zone 2 contains the processes that should be considered for market testing, contracting out or discontinuation.

5

UNDERSTANDING BUSINESS PROCESSES

INTRODUCTION TO BUSINESS PROCESSES

Business processes describe how the work that gets done in an organisation actually gets carried out. Business process analysis then takes this a stage further and looks critically at the work done inside the process, identifies gaps, duplications and dead ends, and finally re-engineers the process to make it more efficient and more responsive to the customers' needs.

The simple definition of a business process is:

- a series of linked activities which take an input from a supplier and produce an output for a customer;
- where an activity is a task or set of tasks which can be described.

The customer of the process is responsible for defining the output of the process and its quality characteristics.

Most non-trivial processes have more than one customer and frequently the output of a process is information.

The simple process model shown in Figure 5.1 describes how this works in practice.

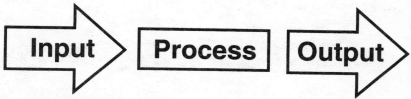

Figure 5.1   *The simple process model.*

Business processes are therefore described in the form of a verb followed by a noun – for example 'billing customers' rather than the noun ' accounts'. Billing customers probably starts at sales and finishes at the bank. Accounts is where someone sits who is part of the 'billing customers' process.

An example of a typical business process in the research and technology organisation described earlier is 'Define product requirements'. This is a complex process that will have many sub-processes which, taken together, will produce the required output – in this case a statement of product requirements.

This process, in common with all other processes, has:

■ a *customer* who receives the output;
■ an *output*, the customer-defined result of the process;
■ a *supplier* who supplies the input;
■ an *input* from which the output is produced;
■ *resources* which are used to produce the output;
■ a *standard* which describes the requirement of the output;
■ *measures* which determine the efficiency and effectiveness of the process;
■ *feedback* to provide information to improve the process.

This can be best illustrated by reference to the process above, 'define product requirements'. Using this as an example:

Customer	– The marketing department
Output	– A new product definition
Supplier	– The technical department
	– Market research
	– Customers
Input	– Technical specifications
	– Marketing window
	– Competitor data
Resources	– Designer
	– Field trials
	– Laboratory tests
Standard	– Due date
	– Test data complete
	– National test results
Measures	– On time achievement
	– Results comparison with competition
Feedback	– Design information
	– Timeliness of information

FLOWCHARTING A PROCESS

Understanding complex processes such as this requires a structure. The first stage of this is flowcharting.

In the same way that a procedure may be considered a description of a process, so a flowchart may serve as a picture of how and when work gets done.

Flowcharting is a simple diagrammatic method of showing the correct sequence in which activities in a series are carried out to produce the required output.

Flowcharting deals with all the features needed to define a process, such as:

- inputs;
- decisions;
- reviews;
- activities;
- documents needed by or produced by the process;
- information needed by the process;
- outputs.

Arrowheads are used to indicate the direction of the sequence of events in the process.

Describing a process in this way promotes a visual common understanding of the process and avoids consideration of unnecessary detail in the first stages of process analysis.

The flowchart allows each step to be given equal importance, ensuring that none are left out. By providing an overview, causes of problems can be seen and what and where to measure can be clarified.

Definition of the inputs and outputs defines the purpose and scope of the process and helps avoid being sidetracked into other areas.

The use of symbols can be very helpful when constructing flowcharts. The most commonly used symbols are shown in Figure 5.2. A simple example of their use in a flowchart is given in Figure 5.3.

When starting a flowchart it is advisable to begin with an overall view with each block of the chart representing a complete department or activity in the organisation. Subsequent work may then take those individual blocks and expand them into lower-level flowcharts. At the next level of chart, various operations would be assigned flowcharts each. This 'breaking down' of the organisation may be continued as far as necessary but, typically, not to the level of individual tasks which are more properly covered by work instructions.

As the process is broken down the 'internal customer' links within the process become clear. These are the internal links with their own inputs and outputs that need to be completed correctly in order to perform the process successfully for the external customer.

Understanding these links and how they work is of major assistance in setting process requirements and then measuring process performance.

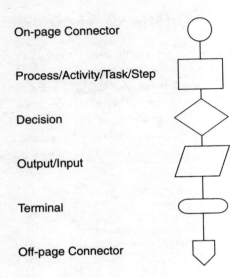

On-page Connector

Process/Activity/Task/Step

Decision

Output/Input

Terminal

Off-page Connector

Figure 5.2 *Flowchart symbols.*

The main benefits of flowcharts are from the provision of:

▪ a simple picture of the process;
▪ a tool for communication to all involved;
▪ an aid for clarification;
▪ a mechanism for deciding what and where to measure;
▪ a tool for challenging the process.

SETTING PROCESS REQUIREMENTS

For a process to be under control, its outputs need to be clearly and concisely defined.

The output must reliably conform to the customer's requirements. However, in many cases, the customer may have insufficient knowledge to indicate the requirements clearly. There must, therefore, be someone inside the organisation with the task of 'process owner' whose role is to listen carefully to the customer and decide what is practicable and will fulfil both the customer's stated and implied needs.

Care must be taken when doing this that the output really does meet the customer's needs, rather than simply specifying what can be produced. In other words, the standard must be 'market driven' rather than product or service led.

An example from the process 'Define product requirements' discussed earlier might be stated as:

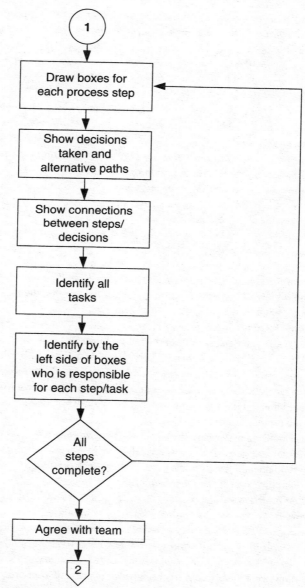

Figure 5.3 *Flowchart symbols in use.*

'To meet the chief product designer on request.'

This might be expressed as:

'To meet the chief product designer on request within 48 hours or a member of the design team on the same day.'

The second statement gives a measurable standard by going beyond the initial requirement and showing how the organisation may meet the customer's needs more completely. Service may not be instantaneous, but will be reliably supplied to the standard specified.

Note how having this dialogue with the customer and agreeing expectations gives both sides a realistic goal.

An example of this in public service has been the arrival of Charter Standards. For example, in the Health Service, 'Where a person is not registered with a GP the FHSA must be able to find a GP for that person within two working days' sets both the process and the service standard.

From the above it can be seen that the responsibility for setting standards lies with those who have the task of meeting those standards.

By continually monitoring process performance and consulting with their customers, process owners may review the standard over time.

It is not beneficial to set standards that are over-harsh and which, in practice, the customers do not want. The effect of this can be a diversion of resources from areas that are important to those that are not, simply because the standard is wrong.

Good definition of a process ensures that each stage is satisfactorily completed before moving onto the next. These stages may themselves have their own output requirements which may in turn be controlled and monitored to ensure that the final output conforms to customer requirements.

Standards should be set to provide clearly defined outputs. They should be as concise as possible, clearly understandable and wholly achievable.

Setting a standard which is obviously unachievable with current processes or resources will fail and will only serve to demotivate the process owner. Clear recognition of the capability of the current process should, therefore, be reflected in the current deliverable standard. Where this standard does not match the customer requirement there is a clear need to revise the process standard.

In the example above, where the chief designer currently responds within three weeks to a request for a meeting he or she is unlikely to achieve a published standard of 48 hours without a fundamental review of the process involved. It is better to begin with reality and move measurably towards the identified goal.

Deciding on the standard is about forming an agreement between the customer and process owner. Where the customer is a single person, office or unit, bilateral discussions may take place. Where more than one person is involved – for example marketing, production, advertising – the full range of views and needs must be accommodated.

Questionnaires and sampling methods are useful, but it is essential that some form of ongoing monitoring is also used to check performance and cope with changing requirements.

There are many processes where both the customer and supplier are internal to the organisation. Here the input to one process is the output from the previous one. Thus the definition of inputs is accomplished with the definition of the previous output. Clearly, these must match. Where the supplier is external to the organisation the process owner should act as the customer and specify his or her input requirements to enable the external supplier to create their own output standards.

This customer–supplier link is often visualised as a chain as in Figure 5.4 with each link in the chain being a process. Clear definition of requirements and standards ensures quality with all stages smoothly interconnecting to satisfy the external customer.

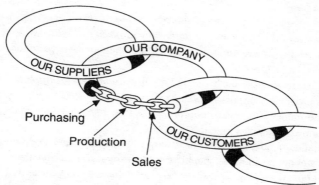

Figure 5.4 *The customer-supplier chain.*

Good, clear process requirements are achieved when they:

■ are not over-long;
■ are clear and concise;
■ meet stated and implied needs;
■ are acceptable to both customer and supplier;
■ are wholly achievable;
■ are capable of being measured;
■ are generated by the marketplace and worked back through the process to the supplier.

MEASURING PROCESS PERFORMANCE

Without some form of measurement it is impossible to gain any objective assessment of performance. For example, a lack of complaints is not a sign that customer requirements are being met. Current capabilities may not be able to provide the performance to meet the process standards that we ultimately might require. Measurement is the only way to plot progress on a path of improvement from the existing to the desired state of affairs.

Within any process there are three distinct areas of measurement:

■ on the input, to ensure that the process is correctly fed;
■ on the process itself, using process success factors to measure process performance;
■ on the output, to enable process measures to be set.

To make sure that measures are proactive rather than reactive they should be set at the most appropriate part of the process rather than simply at the output stage. It is, however, difficult to understand the process measures to use unless the output itself is measured.

It is vital to decide which success factors are critical to achieve the process output standards and then to decide at which point they must be measured – these are the critical measurement points.

The earlier in a process a problem can be identified, the easier it is to resolve, therefore the earlier that meaningful measures can be taken the better. Whenever possible, measures chosen should be simple to collect and should relate as directly as possible to the characteristics being assessed. This allows those directly involved in the process to see the need for corrective action. The more indirect a measure, the more interpretation is necessary before action can be taken.

The more exact a measure the better, but the absence of exact measures should not stop approximate measures being used. Inexact measurement is better than no measurement. In these circumstances it is usually appropriate to take advantage of the security offered by statistics and take samples from the process.

The temptation to take a measurement simply because it is easy to do so, irrespective of whether or not it is meaningful, should be strongly resisted. Probably the most common error made at this stage is that process owners rush off and begin to measure before thinking about what is to be measured.

The most efficient way to set measures on processes is to involve those working directly on the process with the measurement. This is so for three reasons. Firstly, those directly involved probably know more about the operation of the process than experts, so they probably have a better idea of meaningful measures. Secondly, the ownership of the measures will be greater which is necessary in the improvement stage. Lastly, measures set and taken by others are more likely to be challenged and will have little credibility.

There are two distinct elements of measurement:

■ what is actually being measured;
■ how it is expressed.

In all cases the measure is against an agreed standard. The requirements that have been agreed and the standards negotiated must take the capability of the process into account.

The whole point of measurement is quality improvement. In the initial stages we seek to identify and correct those things which cause poor performance. Later we seek to use measurement to raise standards.

INTRODUCTION TO PROCESS ANALYSIS

Process analysis is a technique that builds a fully detailed picture of a process with all the steps clearly identified. From this start point each step in the process is reviewed, allowing problems and areas for improvement to be identified. Process analysis, therefore, gives a systematic approach to process improvement using the power of a team to bring about improvement (Born, 1994).

Process analysis will help you to examine processes in a structured and thorough way so as to improve effectiveness in terms of the above requirements.

For processes to be managed effectively it is necessary to make certain that:

- ▨ customer and supplier requirements are defined, agreed, measured and reviewed;
- ▨ the process is clearly defined;
- ▨ each task within the process has an owner;
- ▨ interfaces are clearly established;
- ▨ process steps are known and understood by those carrying them out;
- ▨ the boundaries between tasks are clear;
- ▨ control points are built into the process;
- ▨ performance measures are in place;
- ▨ there are mechanisms for corrective action.

Process analysis aids the structured examination of a process and enables the above requirements to be put in place.

There is a simple seven-step process to carrying out process analysis.

Step 1: Identify the Process for Analysis

The most important element of this step is to ring fence the process so that you know the start point and the end point. The analysis is then carried out on the process steps in between.

Step 2: Select the Team

The team leader (ideally the process owner) should select a team comprising people with working knowledge of the tasks and details of the process. It is not necessary for each team member to know the complete process in detail, but they must know the steps for which they are the users.

Step 3: Outline Flowcharts

The outline flowchart should illustrate the components which are linked together and make up the total process. It will help you to see the scope of the process and is useful as an 'index' of its elements or components.

The chart should be produced by the team as a whole, pooling all the knowledge, to gain an overall picture of the process as it is today.

Where differences of opinion arise as to how particular elements currently fit together, these must be resolved before further work is undertaken. Talk to other members of the department if necessary.

When agreement is reached on all the elements of the process, the next step may be entered. This involves expanding each step into its detailed flow process.

Step 4: Detailed Flowcharts

This is an important part of the process and care should be exercised in carrying it out.

The object is to produce a detailed and accurate flowchart of each task within the process interlinked to other tasks and activities.

At the end of this exercise, you should be able to identify the inputs and outputs of the process, the routines performed within the process steps and, most importantly, any gaps, duplication, dead ends and inconsistencies.

Each team member should construct the detailed flowchart for their relevant part of the process. These should then be presented to the whole team for awareness and agreement.

Step 5: Task Information Sheets

The purpose of task information sheets is to link the detailed process flow with existing written procedures, controls and system. They will obviously highlight where they do not exist!

When a process is to be changed, the appropriate task information sheet(s) can be used to identify which written procedures and controls will also require change. You will produce one task information sheet for each task.

The following details must be recorded:

- *Process:* the name of the process in which the task is being carried out.
- *Task description:* brief statement of the task which is being carried out. Indicate whether this is manual or automatic.
- *task number:* a unique reference number for each task in the process.
- *Owner:* name of task owner.
- *Department:* owner's department.
- *Skills required:* the skill required to carry out the task, eg keyboard, interpersonal.
- *Media used:* eg paper, magnetic, disc, etc.
- *Standard documents:* any standard documents used.
- *Measurements in place:* the standard performance indicators allocated to the task.
- *Exception control procedures:* how are exceptions or inconsistencies to this process reported and to whom?
- *Dependent tasks:* brief description of any other tasks which are dependent on this one.
- *Observed problems/opportunities:* description of any deficiencies found, or ideas for improvement.
- *Possible action:* note at this stage any potential actions to improve the task. These can be picked up in the next step.

Step 6: Assess the Process

At this point a detailed flowchart is available together with a description of the associated activities. This is used together with the output from Step 4 to enable an assessment to be made of whether:

- the process description is complete;
- there are any dead ends;
- there are any parts of the process duplicated;
- there are any parts of the process that are not needed;
- there are any gaps in the process;
- there are methods for detecting and reporting inconsistencies;
- there are any split responsibilities for simple tasks;
- measurements are relevant and in place.

Step 7: Decide upon Solution

Having completed Step 5 you are now in a position to look at each identified problem in turn and decide upon solutions.

Once a solution has been agreed, insert it into the flowchart and test that the process flow is logical and that no further problems will be caused.

OTHER PROCESS ISSUES

Process Ownership

Documenting a process is often led by an individual or by a small steering group. Much progress can be made in identifying the overall structure of an organisation and in defining the policies and overall goals to be pursued. When documenting the various processes it is essential to involve as many people as practicable. As far as possible, those who do the job should define it. This means that they will take ongoing responsibility for the effective and efficient conduct of the process. It is by being involved that they will identify themselves as owners of the processes. A thorough understanding of the structure will enable them to make changes in the future to meet changing customer requirements.

Involving staff at lower levels in a project such as this carries risk. An individual documenting a task carried out by a number of people may be construed as attempting to 'take charge', thus taking responsibility from the existing organisation structure. Individuals not involved may assume this does not apply to them, or belongs wholly to those directly involved. More dangerous is the documentation of a process which does not match reality.

These barriers may be overcome by involving as many people as possible and ensuring all personnel are kept aware of developments and given suitable training as the need arises.

Process Improvement

The whole concept of measuring quality performance is based on the desire to improve. Most organisations currently run a lot of systems well. All are being required to cover more and/or different tasks on a daily basis. There is a growing emphasis on measurable achievement.

Previously, we looked at documenting how processes operate and how to measure performance. Understanding what needs to be done to make a process work highlights where the problems are and helps show the way to improve. Measurement provides the feedback to assess the impact of changes. Using the process approach concentrates on the system rather than on an individual's performance. All staff are focused on the ultimate aim of satisfying the customer. One weak process in the chain can have disastrous effects.

Once measurable standards are set, it can be seen when they are not met. The reasons for poor performance may be isolated and rectified. Remember to look beyond symptoms to establish root causes.

Where standards are being met, look at the capability of the process. Can a better performance be achieved with the existing structure? Are there any improvements which could be made which would increase capability and allow us to upgrade the standard?

Ideas for improvement should be encouraged from all staff but must be assessed at the correct level of management to determine the benefits and risks involved.

Various problem-solving techniques may be used (Kanji and Asher, 1996):

- brainstorming;
- Pareto analysis;
- cause and effect analysis.

All are directed at working through often complex relationships to define what is truly important to achieve success in the work we do. Understanding the capability of the process is crucial to developing the start point of any improvement process. This may then be compared with benchmarks in other areas or nationally to provide some independent view of performance. Statistics may be used to make comparisons of, for example, prescribing costs, staff costs, turnround times, etc. Histograms and bar charts are useful pictures in this context.

Improvement begins with establishing the status quo. This measured performance may then be assessed against internal or external goals. The areas most ready for improvement may be identified and progressed. Resources must be made available to ensure success. Once the benefits are seen, the improvement process can become an integral part of management with individuals identifying areas for improvement. Ideas may be raised, not as criticisms of poor performance, but as positive suggestions on how to do even better.

USING THE FLOWCHART TO IMPLEMENT PERFORMANCE MEASUREMENT

Through the use of process analysis we have identified the detailed process flowchart together with the internal customers and suppliers and their respective outputs and inputs.

This is now taken a stage further by examining the process flowchart and asking at each step:

What is important at this step?
This could be in the form of a time to complete the step, for example the time to acknowledge a customer complaint. Other possibilities would relate to the accuracy or completeness of the information on a form produced by the process. Perhaps the customer's name is missing or misspelt.

It could be that there is more than one way in which a document can be in error, for example both the address and telephone number could be wrong.

The best way to identify and collect this information is to use a team closely connected with the process and ask them to brainstorm what matters most at the process step.

We then ask at the next step:

What can go wrong?
A complaint can take too long to respond to, letters can be lost or mis-filed, data can be missing off forms for a variety of reasons. We can use cause and effect analysis to help with this stage.

The next question is then:

What can we measure to know if it has gone wrong?
Maybe the time to carry out the first step and the total process time to completion would tell us if things were amiss.

The accuracy of the data collection forms could be measured to look for both incorrect information and missing information.

And then finally:

How can we collect the data?
If we are collecting data on timeliness then a tally chart or checklist would be the correct way to collect the data. We could date stamp the complaint on receipt and then date stamp again on acknowledgement and completion. This would give a simple picture of the timeliness of the response. This is often done by putting a blank stamp on a form on receipt and then progressively filling the information in as follows:

Date received:
Date acknowledged:
Date completed:

This would then travel on the complaint document and the information would be abstracted before final filing and the data collated on a tally chart. (Tally charts are described in Chapter 6.)

Data on accuracy or completeness may involve sampling complaint forms and either counting the number of forms in error or the numbers of errors on forms. Concentration diagrams and checksheets could be the techniques to use here. (Concentration diagrams are also described in Chapter 6.) We could, for example, use a blank copy of the form as a concentration diagram and use it to mark how many times and where errors occurred.

The process flowchart is the basis for the implementation of performance measurement. Whereas in manufacturing industry there is usually a product and that product can be measured, in service or administration there are only processes and the documents or data produced by those processes. Consequently, the flowchart, by describing the process steps and documents produced, is the link from the process itself to the way the process in measured and monitored.

Provided that the process can be flowcharted there should be no real technical problems with measurement. If the process cannot be flowcharted then this is an indication of an ill-defined process and this will need to be remedied before the process can be properly controlled.

The process flowchart shown in Figure 5.5 shows the complete sequence for introducing performance measurement.

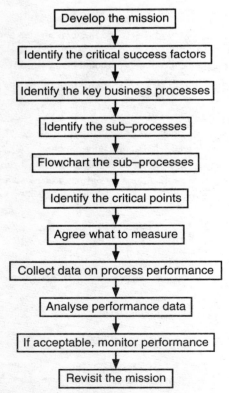

Figure 5.5 *Flowchart for performance measurement.*

6

USING STATISTICS TO MONITOR
PROCESS PERFORMANCE

A fundamental concept of quality improvement is that everything we do is part of a process and that all processes are inherently variable. A key to quality and continuous improvement lies in the reduction of process variability.

Statistical techniques provide both a powerful means of analysing process behaviour and also a common format of displaying process data. They can highlight faults or disturbances that are inherent in the process and indicate where management improvement action is required. The same techniques and charts can then be used to monitor the effect on the process of the corrective actions taken.

Using statistical techniques to improve the process is a cornerstone in the drive to reduce failure costs by increasing investments in prevention. Such techniques indicate if the process is:

- in a state of control or consistent;
- capable of meeting customer requirements.

A positive result on both these scores enables management to minimise or eliminate checking with confidence.

It is through the use of statistical techniques that management can predict the output from any particular process. Management action is therefore directed at preventing problems happening in the first place, rather than directing effort towards detecting problems after the event. It is management's responsibility to lead on all aspects of quality improvement.

The objectives of managing processes must be

- to produce outputs which are consistent over time;
- to produce products and/or services that meet the needs and expectations of the customer;
- to do these two at an economical cost.

It is not sufficient in an organisation to see the objective as simply meeting requirements. This will not lead to the continuous improvement sought, nor will it necessarily satisfy the customer.

INVESTIGATING PROCESS BEHAVIOUR

We now need to understand the performance of the key elements of the process. To achieve this, various statistical tools are available which will be covered in later pages.

The objective of this stage is:

▪ to establish whether the outputs from the process are in a state of statistical control, consistently the same over time, and if not, to eliminate the disturbances which are the cause of inconsistencies;
▪ to establish whether the output is acceptable when the process is in statistical control or consistent. In this case, we monitor it and concentrate on reducing the natural variation in the process. Should the output be consistent but unacceptable then we need to take action to achieve acceptability.

INTRODUCTION TO STATISTICAL TECHNIQUES

Statistics can be defined as the 'collection and arrangement of numerical facts'. It allows predictions to be made about the whole *population* from the analysis of a *sample*. The larger the sample size, the greater the *confidence* we have in our prediction (see, for example, Kume, 1995).

Statistics also help us to describe what is happening to a process or the output from a process pictorially in a way that can be easily understood.

These are not new concepts – insurance companies have used them for many years to predict the length of people's lives and hence calculate the premiums for life insurance.

Mathematicians have developed a wide range of techniques for statistical application and have established a 'common language' for describing the key elements of this subject.

Mathematical statistics in its pure form can be complex and should be left to specialists. However, with a broad understanding of statistical theory and a practical understanding of some simple techniques, everyone can derive considerable benefit from their use.

Statistical process control (SPC) is the name applied to a combination of statistical techniques which are at the heart of total quality, making a fundamental contribution to the achievement of continuous improvement, the prevention of defects and the reduction of the need for expensive inspection systems. These techniques enable us to determine whether or not a process is in a state of 'statistical control', ie consistent and predictable and, if it is, whether or not it is capable of meeting the customer's requirements.

If the process is out of control, ie inconsistent and not predictable, the techniques help to identify the causes of variation, how to eliminate them and how to monitor the process whilst it is brought into a state of control. When the process is in control, SPC techniques are used to monitor the process whilst action is taken to reduce process variation further in an effort to maintain continuous improvement

TECHNIQUES FOR DATA COLLECTION

The most important techniques available are those for data collection and most problems occur at this stage.

As a general point, if data can be collected it can later be analysed. If problems occur in data collection then however sophisticated the analysis it will probably not yield what is being sought.

There is a great temptation, often because of the ease brought about by computers, to collect as much data as possible then to think about it afterwards. This can have the effect of masking what is actually of importance by the sheer volume of data.

The process flowchart is the way into data collection and the flowchart will usually point to what is important in the process, the data to collect to monitor this, where to collect it and then to the relevant technique for data collection.

Data associated with service or administrative processes are usually of two distinct types – data related to process times, ie how long it takes to carry out the process or a subset of the process; and data related to process error, ie the number of failures during the process.

The recommended process for the identification of data to be collected is as follows.

1. Flowchart the process.
2. Identify what is important at each process step.
3. For each of these elements, identify what data is necessary to measure performance.
4. Decide where and how to collect the data.
5. Decide the data collection tool relevant for the data to be collected.

The above five steps are carried out to an optimum by a team of people with knowledge of the process. Brainstorming is one technique that fits in well at this stage.

Concentration Diagrams

Concentration diagrams are used to show the location of events or problems. They are sometimes called *defect location diagrams* or *defect location checksheets*.

Concentration diagrams are useful when seeking to collect data either on process error rates (defectives) or on particular errors occurring within a process (defects). They are used where there is a need to record both frequency and location of an occurrence.

Concentration diagrams are ideal for looking at defects and where they occur. Particular examples are in flowcharts where the location or part of the process in error would be marked on the flowchart, and data recording forms or documents where the location of the error or omission on the document would be marked on the document itself. They are used to illustrate the location of the problem.

Concentration diagrams demonstrate the validity of the proverb: one picture is worth a thousand words. No form of data presentation carries greater conviction.

Some say that concentration diagrams were first used at the time of a cholera outbreak in London, and that a street map was used to identify where people who died of the disease had lived. The concentration of houses around the Broad Street area led to the sealing of a water pump in the area and the subsequent decline of the disease. One outcome of this was the recognition for the first time of epidemiology as a medical discipline.

Whatever the truth of the story, concentration diagrams are one of the most useful and at the same time least used of the data collection tools.

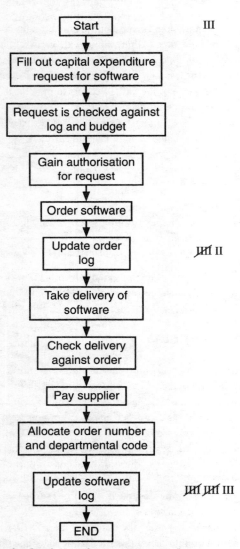

Figure 6.1 *Software log flowchart used as a concentration diagram.*

Two examples of concentration diagrams are given in Figures 6.1 and 6.2.

1. Suppose that you are carrying out a process analysis of one of the processes carried out by your team and that you have drawn a process flowchart to describe it.

   The process flowchart itself can be used as a concentration diagram. When you are examining failures in the process you can mark the 'box' or activity during which the failure occurred. This will give you a count of failures by activity, like that in Figure 6.1.

2. When you are looking for failures that occur in filling in a form, you can use the form itself as a type of checksheet to show concentrations of errors. Figure 6.2 shows an application of this.

MAINTENANCE REQUEST FORM	
Name	
Department	
Department cost code	JHÍ JHÍ JHÍ II
Description of equipment	JHÍ II
Description of fault	JHÍ JHÍ II
Date fault first occurred	
Availability for repair	
Date	
Authorised Signature	
Document 011 Revision 1 Page 1 of 1	

Figure 6.2 *Form used as a concentration diagram.*

The method is to indicate in the box provided each time an error occurs filling in that box. For example, if an error is discovered when someone is filling in item 1 simply place a mark in box 1. The form itself then provides the record of errors.

The process for introducing concentration diagrams is very simple.

▪ *Step 1*. As a group or team you must first decide what data you need.
▪ *Step 2*. Design an individual concentration diagram for people to use as they record the data.
▪ Step 3. *Test the concentration diagram by getting someone who didn't help design it to use it.*
▪ *Step 4*. Make any revisions that are necessary as a result of Step 3.
▪ *Step 5*. Ensure that a master concentration diagram is used to combine the results from the individual forms.
▪ *Step 6*. Proceed to gather the data.

Concentration diagrams are particularly useful in service or administrative functions where it can be difficult otherwise for people to measure and record performance.

Checksheets

A *checksheet* or *tally sheet* is a data recording form that tells you how many times something has happened. Checksheets are usually used for recording numerical data.

In service or administrative processes the most common data collected is process time, either the total time from start to finish of a process or some internal process time. Checksheets would be used to collect this data.

Data reflect facts. Data must be collected carefully and accurately for the results of analysis to have any meaning. Data without a clear purpose or unreliable data is worthless.

Checksheets are all about making data easy to obtain and to use. The main purpose of a checksheet is to compile the data in such a form that it may be used easily and analysed readily.

Checksheets (in an earlier form as tally sticks) were first used in the silk trade to gain a count or tally of the number of bales of silk being transferred to trading vessels in the South China Seas.

They are particularly useful for groups when several people are collecting data. They ensure that everyone will collect comparable data in the same format.

They also provide a clear record of gathered data. There are as many different designs of checksheets as there are reasons for collecting data. The important thing is to design a checksheet to suit the data being collected.

Use a 'five-bar gate' to record the number of errors found, as shown in Figure 6.3.

Again, the process for introducing checksheets is very simple.

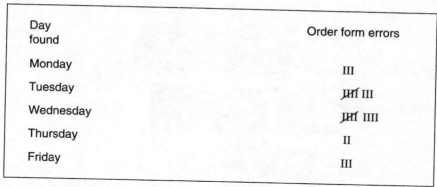

Day found	Order form errors
Monday	III
Tuesday	JHT III
Wednesday	JHT IIII
Thursday	II
Friday	III

Figure 6.3 *Checksheet of order form errors by day of the week.*

■ *Step 1.* As a group or team you must first decide what data you need. Brainstorming and cause and effect analysis are useful ways of determining this information. You are trying to answer two questions:
  – Will the data gathered reveal the facts?
  – Can the data be analysed in such a way as to reveal the facts?
■ *Step 2.* Design an individual checksheet form for people to use as they record the data. This sheet must reflect the type of data being collected.
■ *Step 3.* Test the checksheet by getting someone who didn't help design it to use it.
■ *Step 4.* Make any revisions that are necessary as a result of Step 3.
■ *Step 5.* Many people are going to use the checksheet to collect data. You must design a master checksheet to combine the results from the individual forms.
■ *Step 6.* Proceed to gather data.

It is important to take action according to the data and to get into the habit of discussing problems based on fact.

TECHNIQUES FOR DATA ANALYSIS

Once we have collected data on process performance we seek to analyse that data to look for patterns that will give further information about the process.

Again, the simplest techniques are the most useful.

Bar Charts and Histograms

A *bar chart*, as in Figure 6.4, is a graphical method of showing the differences between various discrete categories of data.

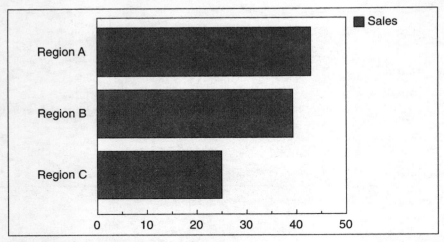

Figure 6.4 *Bar chart of regional sales figures.*

A *histogram,* as in Figure 6.5, is used to show how data is spread across a continuous range of values.

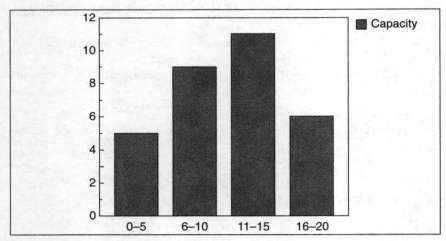

Figure 6.5 *Histogram of office capacity.*

A *bar chart* shows a comparison between different categories. For example, the sales in different regions could be shown on a bar chart as in Figure 6.6 to give a comparison between the regions.

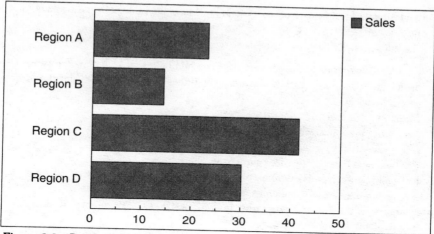

Figure 6.6 *Bar chart of sales.*

The bar chart shows that sales are best in Region C and worst in Region B. Using this information the regions could be further investigated to see why this variation should occur.

The histogram is used when data is spread across a continuous range of values. This is sometimes called a *frequency distribution*.

The histogram illustrated in Figure 6.7 shows the frequency and ages of employees in a typical organisation. It shows that 5 per cent of employees are aged between 45 and 49 and 5 per cent are aged under 20. Although this information can be presented in various ways, the histogram gives a graphical indication of staff ages.

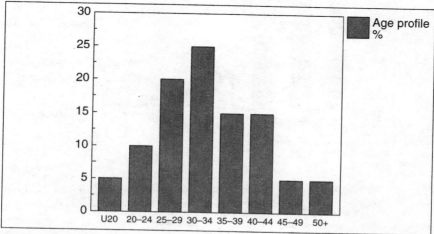

Figure 6.7 *Histogram of employee ages.*

In a histogram it is the area of the bar that represents the value of the data and not just the height.

The rules for bar charts and histograms are as follows:

■ Decide on your scale – it needs to make sense and be readable. You don't want bars the length of the page – they would look silly. If they are too short it's difficult to compare differences.
■ Mark out your axes.
■ Make sure the x axis will take all of your bars.
■ Make sure all of your bars are the same width.
■ Put bars next to each other for comparison.
■ Put a gap between pairs or groups of bars – multi-columns as they are called – to make it easy to separate each time unit's figures.
■ Always start the y axis at zero rather than 50 or 100 since it can mislead the reader into thinking the numbers are only small.
■ Shade your bars – especially multi-columns – to help the reader pick them out.
■ Label both axes.

As well as giving a pictorial representation of the data, analysis of histograms can reveal what is actually happening in some office situations.

The histogram in Figure 6.8 shows office production figures for claims processing. The cliff shape at the left-hand side suggests that the data is being tampered with in some way and that figures below 20 are being censored. It would be highly unlikely that, given a normal distribution of the figures, there would be no figures below 20.

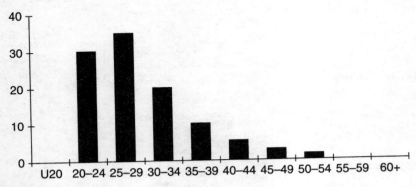

Figure 6.8 *Histogram of office productivity.*

Similarly the histogram in Figure 6.9 exhibits a comb-like shape with an up-and-down appearance. The most likely explanation of this shape is a mixture of working methods or practices between offices or shifts, with one office being consistently ahead of the other in terms of output.

Both of these patterns are deserving of investigation. You have discovered additional information and it is worthwhile finding out more.

- In Figure 6.8 where is the missing data?
- In Figure 6.9 can the better performing unit pass on how they achieve this to the other?

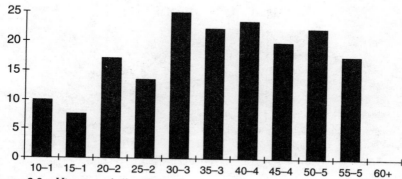

Figure 6.9 *Histogram of office productivity.*

Pareto Analysis

Pareto analysis is a technique for recording and analysing information relating to a problem or cause, which easily enables the most significant aspects to be identified.

A Pareto diagram is a special form of bar chart which allows the information to be visually displayed.

Analysis often reveals that, for example, a small number of failures are responsible for the bulk of quality costs. This conforms to the so-called 'Pareto principle', named after the Italian economist who discovered that the majority of his country's wealth was owned by relatively few people.

In many situations a similar pattern becomes apparent when we look at the relationship between numbers of items and their contribution to the extent of the problem. This pattern has been referred to as the 80/20 rule (see Figure 6.10) and shows itself in many ways. For instance, 80 per cent of your telephone calls come from 20 per cent of your colleagues; similarly 80 per cent of a company's failure costs probably result from 20 per cent of its problem areas.

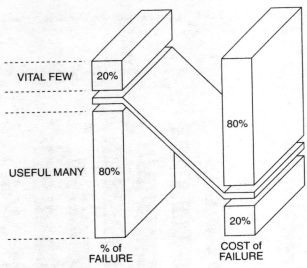

Figure 6.10 *The Pareto principle, or the 80/20 rule.*

The 80/20 principle does not mean that exactly 80 per cent of the total problem is provided for by 20 per cent of the features but that there is usually a similarly large imbalance. The ratio itself is not as important as the fact that it is the major causes that are being identified.

In other words, amongst the wide range of problems that you may be faced with, there are a few vital ones which must be tackled immediately and many others which can be dealt with later. Pareto analysis shows at a glance which problem areas can be regarded as the vital few needing special measures to tackle them, and which are the useful many.

'First things first' is the thought behind the Pareto diagram; the properly constructed diagram should suggest on which error or activity resources should be used first to make the best improvement.

Very often the simple process of arranging data may suggest something of importance that would otherwise have gone unnoticed. Selecting classifications, tabulating data, ordering data and constructing the Pareto diagram have often served a useful purpose in problem investigation.

The steps required to construct a Pareto diagram are as follows:

■ *Step 1*. List activities or errors to be analysed and place in Column 1.
■ *Step 2*. Count how often they occur and place in Column 2.
■ *Step 3*. Calculate the total for Column 2 and the percentage that each item represents of this total (Column 3).
■ *Step 4*. Order totals, starting with the largest, and calculate the cumulative percentage as you go down the list (Column 4).

Having completed Steps 1–4 your table should look as follows:

Error (1)	Frequency (2)	% of total (3)	Running % (4)
Typing error	42	36	36
Spelling mistake	35	30	66
Grammar	24	21	87
Illegible	12	10	97
Poor layout	4	3	100
Total	117	100	

▪ *Step 5*. Draw the Pareto diagram using the figures in Column 3 as shown in Figure 6.11.

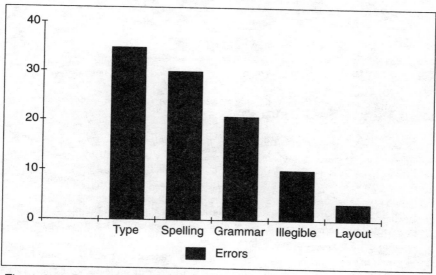

Figure 6.11 *Pareto diagram of reasons for errors.*

The Pareto diagram can be enhanced by drawing the cumulative curve using the figures taken from Column 4, as shown in Figure 6.12. The curve is completed by joining the top right-hand corner of each bar of the cumulative bar chart thus produced.

▪ *Step 6*. Interpret results.

The candidates for priority action, the 'vital few', will appear on the left of the Pareto diagram where the slope of the cumulative curve will be steepest.

The 'useful many' should not be ignored. Sometimes an apparent triviality now can become significant later. It is important to examine the 'useful many' for any such 'time bombs'.

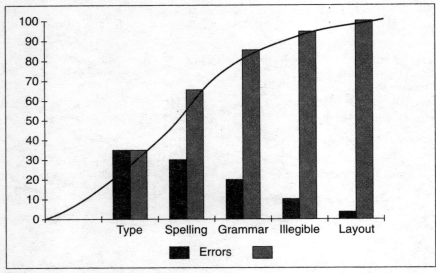

Figure 6.12 *Cumulative Pareto diagram.*

Cause and Effect Diagrams

Cause and effect diagrams, also known as *fishbone* or *Ishikawa diagrams*, are a means of identifying and organising possible causes of a problem. It is a visually effective way of recording data and makes it easy to see relationships between causes.

A cause and effect (or fishbone) diagram is constructed in three stages.

▪ First, establish what the problem or effect is. Start the diagram by putting this in a box.
▪ Next, attempt to identify major causes. Put these in boxes on branches of the fishbone. (Figure 6.13 shows how this is done.)
▪ We then brainstorm for subdivisions of the major causes. If what was thought to be a minor cause turns out to be more significant, redraw the diagram accordingly. If a particular cause has a large number of sub-causes, it is useful to turn it into a separate diagram.

To focus discussion, we circle the most likely causes and draw lines to indicate the relationship between them.

Cause and effect diagrams help detailed investigation of processes responsible for problems. They provide a convenient way of revealing relationships between causes, and can help in defining the problem more closely.

Follow these ground rules to ensure the technique works effectively:

▪ Use large diagrams. You can't expect people to participate if they can't see what is going on.
▪ Look out for and examine closely the relationships between causes – this is where unexpected solutions are likely to turn up.

▪ If you start to become overwhelmed with causes, you haven't defined the problem closely enough and must go back to the first stage.
▪ Remember, the aim is not to apportion blame but to understand the problem well enough to propose effective solutions.

Figure 6.13 shows a cause and effect diagram drawn by a team trying to establish why people missed a training course.

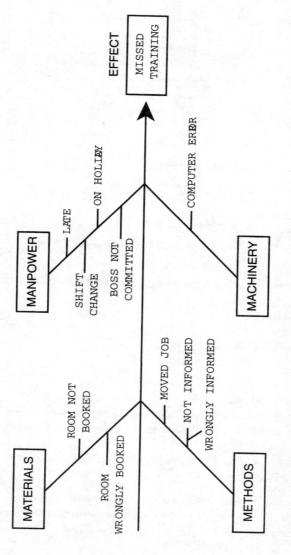

Figure 6.13 *Cause and effect diagram of reasons for missing training.*

SIMPLE STATISTICAL MEASURES

A statistic is a measurement that allows us to describe some property of a distribution.

We may be interested in the average time to process an application or in the spread of times, ie the difference between the longest and shortest time. Both of these simple descriptive statistics enable a picture to be painted of what is happening in the processes that we manage.

Measures of Location

The most common measure of location used in statistics is the *mean*.

The Mean

$$\text{Mean} = \text{ordinary arithmetic average}$$
$$= x \text{ bar (as spoken)}$$
$$= \bar{x} \text{ (as written)}$$
$$= \frac{\Sigma x}{n}$$

where n = sample size
x = a value in the sample
Σx = sum of x values.

Example: Find the mean value of 6, 8, 3, 3, 5.

$$\text{Mean} = \frac{6 + 8 + 3 + 3 + 5}{5} = \frac{25}{5} = 5$$

This measure makes intrinsic sense – it simply represents the average of the numbers in the group.

Measures of Spread

The Range

The *range* indicates the spread of the extreme values. It is calculated by taking the smallest value in the sample from the largest value, and is represented by the symbol R.

In the above example the largest value was 8 and the smallest 3 so the range would be $8 - 3 = 5$.

Standard Deviation

Although the range is an easy way to measure the amount of variation in a set of values it has a drawback. The range only takes into account the extreme values and disregards all other information contained in the data.

To overcome this drawback, statisticians use the *standard deviation* as the preferred measure of spread

Standard deviation is a measure which reflects the variability and dispersion of a process. The greater the variability, the greater is the standard deviation.

Standard deviation is represented by the symbols 's' or σ (sigma) and is calculated from:

$$s = \frac{\sqrt{(x_i - \bar{x})^2}}{n-1}$$

Rarely do we use this formula since the advent of scientific calculators has eliminated the need for tedious manual calculation.

The Standard Deviation and Prediction

The distribution most frequently encountered in industrial and commercial processes and also in nature is the *normal* (or *Gaussian*) *distribution*. This is important because knowledge of the properties of the normal distribution enable us to make predictions about machine and process performance. A normal distribution appears graphically as a symmetrical, bell-shaped curve, as shown in Figure 6.14.

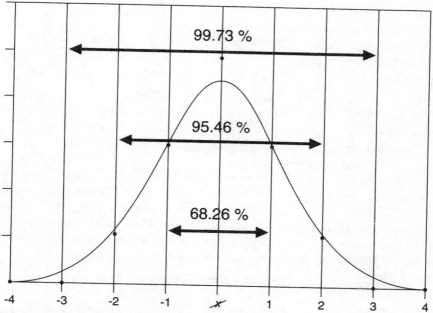

Figure 6.14 *The normal curve.*

If the mean $\bar{x}$ and standard deviation s of a normally distributed sample are known it is possible to predict the proportion of the population that will fall between any two limits.

For instance, as shown, any normal distribution will have 68.26 per cent of the population in the area under the curve between one standard deviation above and below the mean. This area would be referred to as 1s. The area within 2s is 95.44 per cent of the total, within 3s is 99.73 per cent and within 4s is 99.994 per cent.

Other important percentages can also be noted. For instance 0.135 per cent would be above +3s, leaving 99.865 per cent below that same point. For distributions other than the normal, these percentages would be different, but the basic concept would be the same.

The mean and standard deviation of a total population can be estimated from measurements on a small number of items, so we can *predict* the proportion of the population within any particular limits. When the data measurements are taken from a sample of the output of a machine or process, we can predict the distribution of all of the output of that machine or process, and assess its relation to the specification.

DIFFERENT TYPES OF PROCESS VARIATION

No two service deliveries are ever exactly alike. The differences may be large, or they may be very small, but they are always present. The time to process a complaint, for instance, would be affected by:

▪ equipment (availability of word processor);
▪ environment (tidiness);
▪ administration (training);
▪ methods (backlog).

The many differences resulting from the combined effect of these influences are known as *variation*. Variation also exists in management processes and systems and can be monitored using the same techniques.

To be of good quality, the outputs of a process must conform with some predetermined specifications and they must be consistent.

Traditional quality controls are designed only with the first requirement in mind; statistical process control takes account of the need for consistency. Perfect consistency is not attainable; all processes are subject to disturbances which cause variability in their outputs.

To manage any process the variation must be reduced by tracing it back to its source. The first step is to make the distinction between common and special causes of variation, otherwise known as *common* and *special disturbances*.

▪ *Common disturbances*. These cause process variation that leads to service variability which is predictable and characteristic of the process. They are disturbances from natural causes that occur randomly and are always present when a process is in operation.
▪ *Special disturbances*. These cause process variation and service variability which is not predictable. They arise from causes that are not inherent in the process, eg the weather, differences in forms.

When statistical process control is first applied, special disturbances must be identified and eliminated, so that the process is brought to a predictable condition, ie to a 'state of statistical control'. At this stage, common disturbances can be identified and reduced. If new special disturbances are introduced, they take the process out of control and must be eliminated before dealing further with common disturbances.

To find special and common disturbances, we first have to produce control charts. By interpreting a control chart we can separate special and common disturbances by seeing if the process is in a state of statistical control (consistent) or not (inconsistent).

7

INTRODUCTION TO CONTROL CHARTS

Control charts take the static picture that a frequency distribution portrays and show the time relationship. Control charts provide immediate feedback about the *behaviour* of a process. The nature of the feedback provided by control charts allows one to distinguish between operationally caused variations and system-caused variations. Control charts are a type of graph which provides a *running* picture of what is happening to a process.

The relationship with histograms is simple. The histogram gives a snapshot, balance sheet or picture of what a process *has done*; the control chart gives a moving picture, a video, of what a process *is doing* in real time.

USES OF CONTROL CHARTS

Since control charts provide continuous monitoring of what is occurring, they are used to control the process by helping to detect when the statistical variations indicate that something other than common causes are occurring to the materials, equipment, methods, people or environment. The data from a control chart is a record of a process. Control charts are used to:

- diagnose problems by signalling that a process is out of control so that corrective actions can be taken immediately.
- understand when to leave a process alone and thus avoid unnecessarily frequent adjustment which tends to increase the variability of a process, rather than decrease it.
- determine the inherent capability of a process.

TYPES OF CONTROL CHARTS

There are two types of data to which statistical techniques can be applied:

- *Variable data:* where a characteristic of a process or output can be measured in terms of values on a continuous scale. The most usual type of variable data in service processes is time.
- *Attribute data:* where a characteristic is appraised in terms of whether it meets or does not meet a given requirement, eg good/bad, go/no go, pass/fail. In service processes this is usually either error in processes, that is, process failure, or errors in processes, documents, etc.

Control charts are available to handle both types of data.

Variable Data Control Charts

Variable data control charts are used to control the variation of processes in cases where the characteristic under investigation is a measurable quantity, usually process time.

The following are two types of variable data control charts in common use:

- mean and range charts ($\bar{x}$ and R);
- moving range charts (xMR).

Chapters 8 and 9 explain the construction of mean and range charts and the moving range chart in detail.

The main advantage of $\bar{x}$ and R control charts is that you obtain specific data about a single characteristic of a process thereby providing clues as to the problem, whereas as with an attribute control chart you only determine whether the process or product is under control or not. Moreover, with an attribute control chart, any attribute of the service may be the problem, but with $\bar{x}$ and R charts, you control the specific attributes you are measuring.

The disadvantage of $\bar{x}$ and R control charts is that there may be many variables to be measured (for example intermediate process times) and to watch all of these would require many separate $\bar{x}$ and R control charts – one for every variable thought to be important. This can be very costly, so usually a mix of both variable and attribute control charts are used.

Attribute Data Control Charts

In many areas, the nature of the process makes it impossible to collect measured data. Such processes include typing and raising invoices. Where precise measurement is not possible, there is usually qualitative information about process attributes; this amounts to 'yes' or 'no' against some predetermined standard.

If this information is used in an attribute data control chart, it can be used to get an idea of the spread and variation of the process.

Where process or service characteristics can be measured, process control should be carried out by using variables. Variable data control charts show the degree of variation, require smaller sample sizes and are more precise.

When charting attributes, two distinct types of data should be recognised:

- *defectives* which are outputs that fail to meet a required standard due to the presence of defects;
- *defects* which are faults (or non-conforming characteristics) that cause outputs to fail to meet a required standard, eg errors on an order form.

There may be more than one defect in a defective item.

There are four main types of attribute data control charts:

- proportion defective (*p*) charts;
- number defective (*np*) charts;
- number of defects (*c*) charts;
- number of defects per unit (*u*) charts.

An explanation and examples of each of these types of attribute data control chart are provided in Chapter 12.

8

THE CONSTRUCTION OF $\bar{x}$ AND R CHARTS

When we are monitoring a process by using a measurement, for example timeliness, the type of chart to use could be the $\bar{x}$ and R charts.

$\bar{x}$ and R charts are used as a pair; they are constructed from measurements of the particular characteristic under investigation, ie the variable. In service and administration areas this is often either total process time or intermediate times.

DATA COLLECTION

Data is collected in small samples of constant size, usually five consecutive items, that are drawn periodically (eg every 15 minutes, daily). The data gathering plan must specify how this is to be carried out.

How Many Items in the Sample?

It is important to choose a sample size that offers a minimum opportunity for variation within the sample. For an initial study, between four and 16 consecutive outputs should be used as a sample.

All the items should have been produced under similar conditions within a short time so that variations within the sample will tend to reflect only common disturbances.

How Often Should the Sample be Taken?

Subject to economic considerations, samples should be taken so that changes in the process over time can be detected quickly. Existing data might be used, if available, to establish the sampling frequency in cases where time to time variation is present.

Potential causes of time variation can be detected by sampling at regular intervals, but care must be taken to minimise bias, by avoiding a definite checking time such as on the hour.

Normally, when a control chart is first applied, samples for the initial study are taken frequently. After the process has been brought into control and improvements have been made, the frequency tends to decrease. Then, only enough checks are made to ensure the maintenance of control.

Sufficient samples should be taken to allow time for all major disturbances to appear. A minimum of 25 samples (each of five consecutively produced individual samples) might be necessary to enable good estimates of the process spread and location to be made.

RECORDING THE DATA

The individual measurements for each sample are recorded and the following parameters are calculated:

Mean $\bar{x}$ the sum of the individual values, divided by the total number in the sample.

Range R the difference between the largest and the smallest individual value in each sample.

The data below gives hourly values for the number of forms processed, taken five times a day for 20 days:

Sample number						Total X	Mean $\bar{x}$	Range
1	27	25	24	23	21	120	24.0	6
2	22	22	24	22	22	112	22.4	2
3	21	21	22	21	22	107	21.4	1
4	26	25	25	23	21	120	24.4	5
5	23	22	21	23	23	112	22.4	5
6	23	26	28	24	26	125	25.0	5
7	23	27	28	24	26	125	25.0	5
8	28	26	26	24	24	128	25.6	4
9	25	22	21	26	23	117	23.4	5
10	21	26	25	23	20	115	23.0	6
11	21	21	22	21	22	107	21.4	1
12	27	25	24	23	21	120	24.0	6
13	22	22	24	22	22	112	22.4	2
14	21	21	22	21	22	107	21.4	1
15	23	27	28	24	26	125	25.0	5
16	28	26	26	24	24	128	25.6	4
17	25	22	21	26	23	117	23.4	5
18	23	25	24	23	21	116	23.2	4
19	26	24	21	22	22	115	23.0	5
20	21	26	25	23	20	115	23.0	6
Total							469	83
Mean							23.45	4.15

The calculated means and ranges are then plotted on the control charts to show patterns and trends, as shown in Figures 8.1 and 8.2.

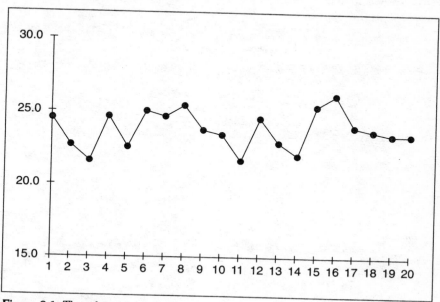

Figure 8.1 *The x̄ chart*

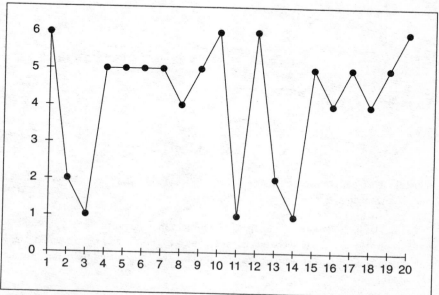

Figure 8.2 *The R chart*

THE MEAN RANGE AND PROCESS MEAN

Two parameters are then calculated from the data and are drawn on the chart as horizontal lines, as in Figures 8.3 and 8.4.

Mean range $\overline{R}$ The sum of all the sample ranges, divided by the total number of samples. This is called $\overline{R}$.

Process mean $\overline{\overline{x}}$ The sum of all the sample means, divided by the total number of samples. This is called $\overline{\overline{x}}$.

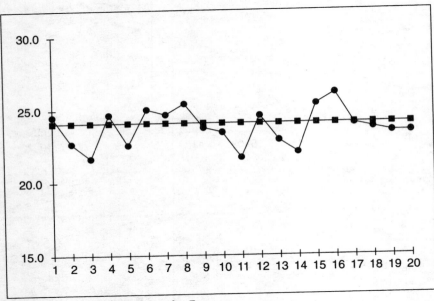

Figure 8.3 *The $\overline{x}$ chart with centre line $\overline{\overline{x}}$*

CONTROL LIMITS

The difference between control charts and any other kind of graph is that they contain a centre line and an upper and lower control line. These three lines are calculated from data generated by the process.

Control limits are constructed on the chart to establish if the process is in a state of statistical control or not. They show the extent to which the means and ranges would vary if only common disturbances were present. Control limits are calculated using the formulae shown opposite.

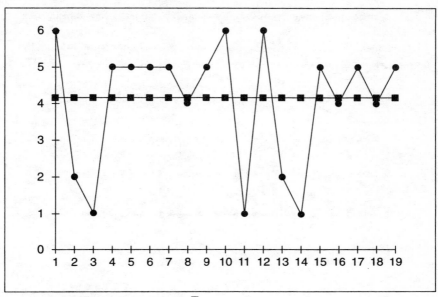

Figure 8.4 *The R chart with centre line $\bar{R}$*

Mean chart upper control limit:
$$UCL_x = \bar{\bar{x}} + A_2 \times \bar{R}$$
$$\text{So } UCL_x = 23.45 + 0.58 \times 4.15$$
$$= 25.86$$

Mean chart lower control limit:
$$LCL_x = \bar{\bar{x}} + A_2 \times \bar{R}$$
$$\text{So } LCL_x = 23.45 - 0.58 \times 4.15$$
$$= 21.04$$

Range chart upper control limit:
$$UCL_R = D_4 \times \bar{R}$$
$$\text{So } UCL_R = 2.11 \times 4.15$$
$$= 8.76$$

Range chart lower control limit:
$$LCL_R = D_3 \times \bar{R}$$
$$\text{So } LCL_R = 0$$

In these formulae A_2, D_3 and D_4 are constants whose values depend upon the sample size and are obtained from statistical tables given in Appendix 3.

The upper control limit represents three standard deviations and is sometimes called the *action line*.

Control limits are drawn as solid horizontal lines, as shown in Figures 8.5 and 8.6.

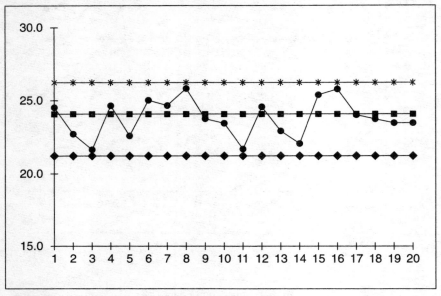

Figure 8.5 *The x̄ chart with centre line and control limits.*

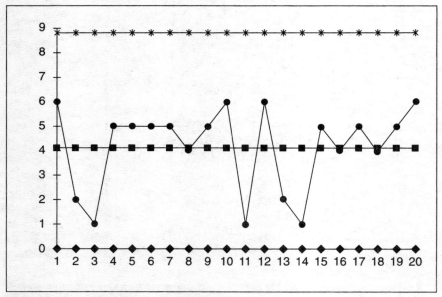

Figure 8.6 *The R chart with centre line and control limits.*

CONTROL CHART INTERPRETATION

Chart Examination and Analysis

A control chart helps to identify whether a process is in a state of statistical control. This means that the process is stable and predictable and that the causes of variation are due only to common disturbances within the process. Special disturbances might be present and they must be eliminated to achieve a state of statistical control. Once control has been achieved, the quality of the service can be predicted, and changes to the process become worthwhile and cost effective.

Charts are examined to detect out-of-control situations; the two parts of the chart (ie mean and range, mean and standard deviation) are examined both separately and jointly to help deduce when special disturbances are or are not affecting the process.

It is important to realise that by taking means of several values and plotting those means together with a centre line and two control limits, all decisions are then taken on the basis of the mean value plotted. We lose the ability to react to any particular individual value that might itself cause concern.

It is easy to see that the individual values will be more spread than the means and it could be the case that individual values might fall outside the control limits whilst the mean of those values does not.

When this happens we interpret the chart according to the mean value plotted. To do otherwise and react to the individual value moves away from the statistics that govern the control chart and will result in making changes to the process when none are needed – in other words, overreacting.

The R chart will, in any case, pick up any major changes to the process range.

Interpreting $\bar{x}$ and R Charts

The range chart is analysed first. When the ranges are in a state of statistical control, the process spread within the sample variation is accepted as being stable.

The order of interpretation is important. The process is unstable and out of statistical control if the $\bar{x}$ chart is within the limits but the range chart is not. The range chart will tell you if special causes are present.

If the range chart is acceptable you then interpret the $\bar{x}$ chart. If it is not, there is no reason to interpret the $\bar{x}$ chart as you already know that the process is out of statistical control.

The mean chart is analysed second to determine if the process mean is changing with time. If the means are in control, changes in location represent common disturbances; if the means are not in control, there are probably special disturbances present, which are making the process location unstable. Making alterations to the process under these circumstances would be a waste of time; it could actually increase the number of defects.

For each out of control situation, an analysis of the operation of the process should be conducted to determine the reason for the special disturbance. The process can be brought into control only by individuals taking effective action to remove special disturbances and obtain a state of statistical control. Steps must be taken to ensure that improvements made by this action are permanently maintained.

Points outside the control limits on $\bar{x}$ and R charts could indicate one or more of the following:

Range chart:
▨ control limit or point miscalculated or misplotted;
▨ measurement system changed (eg a different manager);
▨ item-to-item variability or spread of the process has changed.

Mean chart:
▨ control limit or point miscalculated or misplotted;
▨ measurement system has changed;
▨ process has shifted, either at an isolated point in time or as part of a trend.

Patterns within the Limits

Even when all plotted points fall within the control limits, there may be patterns which could be indications of special disturbances that influence the consistency of products. These patterns should be investigated, because they indicate a process shift that might lead to drift beyond the control limits and, consequently, unacceptable products.

▨ A process in a state of statistical control, subject only to common disturbances, will have points distributed randomly about the process mean.
▨ Seven successive points that all fall above or below the mean are an indication of a process drift. The process is then *not* in a state of statistical control.
▨ Eight successive plotted points in an upward or downward direction indicate a change in process spread on a range chart and in process location on a mean chart. The process is then *not* in a state of statistical control.
▨ When there are more than 90 per cent of points in the middle third of the band between the control limits then the process is *not* in a state of statistical control. This could mean:
  – control limits or individual points have been miscalculated or misplotted;
  – the process or sampling method is stratified. Each subgroup contains measurements from two or more process streams that have different average performances (eg the mixed output of two sales departments);
  – the data has been edited by values that would have deviated from the average being altered or removed;
  – the process has improved and the control limits needs recalculating.
▨ When there are less than 40 per cent of points in the middle third of the band between control limits, then the process is *not* in a state of statistical control. This could mean:

  – calculation or plotting errors have been made;

– the process sampling method causes successive sub-groups to contain measurements from two different sales offices.

More specifically for $\bar{x}$ and R charts, a pattern in a range chart could indicate a change in the process spread that might have been caused by changes in materials, methods, etc. On a mean chart, a pattern could indicate a change in the process location that might have been caused by fatigue, equipment wear or gradual changes in the environment.

Examples of the uses of $\bar{x}$ and R charts include

- uses of photocopier paper;
- telephone usage;
- average weekly claims processing times;
- computer response times.

There are occasions when, for whatever reason, it is only possible to collect one data point. When this is so the type of variable chart drawn is the $\bar{x}$ moving range chart covered in the next chapter.

THE x MOVING RANGE CHART

$\bar{x}$ and R charts depend on samples of a predetermined size, usually five, taken from the process at regular intervals. The mean value is calculated and plotted and the information provided by the samples is then used to determine the state of the process from which they are taken.

This approach is used whenever the number of items generated by the process is so large that individual items cannot economically or effectively be assessed. A typical example is in checking five invoices or claim forms per day out of, say, the 200 or so which are being produced.

There are many cases where the numbers involved are much smaller and individual readings become possible. An example of this would be data generated by a design and build process in an architects' practice where very few different buildings are commissioned. Profit and loss statements and other monthly or quarterly management accounts data provide ideal figures which can be charted as single readings. In other words, there is only one figure available.

This data has to be handled differently from that when there was a multiple sample size. The type of control chart used is called the x moving range chart.

Data of this kind is generated routinely by most accounts departments and is in fact published monthly by the Central Statistical Office showing the performance of the UK economy over the past months and quarters.

The normal thing is for the data to be published and then for a series of pundits to seek to draw conclusions from the latest figures. This is invariably done in isolation from the historical data and takes no account of the variability of the data.

The following data shows the weekly production figures from a claims underwriting process for the first 12 weeks of the financial year.

Week	Value £m
1	3.585
2	3.549
3	3.515
4	3.495
5	3.579
6	3.487
7	3.480
8	3.533
9	3.499
10	3.563
11	3.551
12	3.389

Data in this format is very difficult to interpret and the natural approach is to compare the latest figure with the one before. Is it higher? Is it lower? What conclusions are possible? It should be obvious that the figures will normally be different so there will always be plenty to argue about.

The tendency is therefore to react to figures as they come along and develop 'gut feel'. This usually results in overreaction followed by a reaction the opposite way the following month when the next set of figures is available. The organisation will then swing from one way of operating to another, so increasing the overall variability.

CALCULATING THE MOVING RANGE

The first step in drawing the x moving range chart is to artificially generate a range by subtracting the successive x values from each other, as shown below:

Week	Value £m	Moving range
1	3.585	–
2	3.549	0.036
3	3.515	0.034
4	3.495	0.020
5	3.579	0.116
6	3.487	0.092
7	3.480	0.007
8	3.533	0.053
9	3.499	0.034
10	3.563	0.064
11	3.551	0.012
12	3.389	0.048

There are two things to note. Firstly, there can be no moving range value for the first x value, so there is always one fewer moving range values than there are x values. Secondly, if the value obtained is negative then the negative sign is dropped.

As with the $\bar{x}$ and R charts, we then add together the x values and the moving range (MR) values, as follows:

Week	Value £m	Moving range
1	3.585	–
2	3.549	0.036
3	3.515	0.034
4	3.495	0.020
5	3.579	0.116
6	3.487	0.092
7	3.480	0.007
8	3.533	0.053
9	3.499	0.034
10	3.563	0.064
11	3.551	0.012
12	3.389	0.048
Total	42.225	0.516

CALCULATING THE CENTRE LINES

The centre line for the x chart, $\bar{x}$, is then:

$$\bar{x} = \frac{\Sigma x}{12} = \frac{42.225}{12} = 3.519$$

and the centre line for the moving range chart is:

$$\bar{R} = \frac{\Sigma MR}{11} = \frac{0.516}{11} = 0.047$$

As before we calculate the control limits.

CALCULATING THE CONTROL LIMITS

Control Limits for x

As with all control charts, control limits are set at three standard deviations on either side of the central line. The calculation used here is different from that used when dealing with samples.

We obtain the standard deviation directly from the relationship $s = \bar{R}/d_2$, where d_2 is a constant given in the table in Appendix 3.

Since we are grouping the x values consecutively in pairs we use d_2 for a sample size of two.

R/d_2 is defined as an estimate of the standard deviation, but based on the moving range R rather than the individual reading x.

So:

$$UCL_x = \bar{x} + \frac{3R}{d_2}$$

$$= \bar{x} + 3 \times \frac{0.047}{1.128}$$

$$= 3.519 + 0.125$$

$$= 3.644$$

and

$$LCL_x = \bar{x} - \frac{3\bar{R}}{d_2}$$

$$= \bar{x} - 3 \times \frac{0.047}{1.128}$$

$$= 3.519 - 0.125$$

$$= 3.394$$

Control Limits for *R*

Control limits for R use D_3 and D_4 constants as before. The only difference is that the sample size is two, not five, since we have artificially generated a sample size of two.

So:

$$UCL_R = D_4 R$$

$$= 3.267 \times 0.047$$

$$= 0.154$$

$$LCL_R = D_3 R \text{ which is 0 as } D_3 = 0$$

The two charts are then drawn, as shown in Figures 9.1 and 9.2.

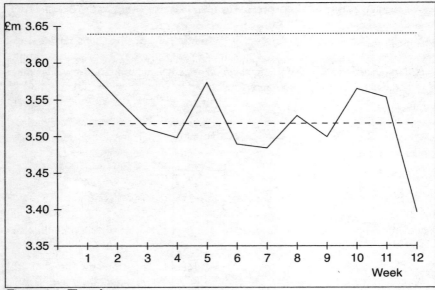

Figure 9.1 *The x chart.*

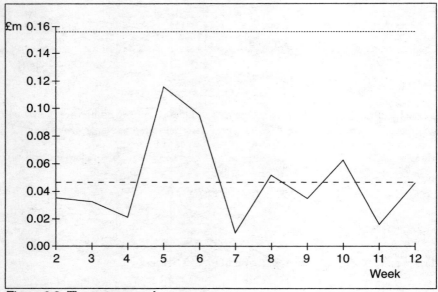

Figure 9.2 *The moving range chart.*

INTERPRETING THE *x* MOVING RANGE CHART

The range chart is interpreted as before. As seen here the chart is in control. Applying the rules for detecting special causes shows that the *x* chart went out of control on the last week when the value of £3.389 m was below the control limit of £3.394 m. Action would then be taken to investigate and find out why this was the case.

The major benefit of using statistically based charts in a situation like this is that they bring with them a clear set of guidelines as to when we should or should not react to a reading. By doing this we avoid the waste of effort that often comes from attempting to explain away numbers that actually only represent random variation within a process.

SOME APPLICATIONS OF *x* MOVING RANGE CHARTS

Many applications in service and administration involve time. These include the times taken to:

- respond to a complaint or query;
- issue an insurance cover note;
- deal with a claim;
- produce a quotation;
- respond to an enquiry;
- process a letter of credit;
- issue an invoice.

Other applications that are not time based include:

- sales expenses;
- monthly sales figures;
- accounting information;
- average weekly unprocessed cash;
- stock or inventory levels.

Many of the above could equally be measured in terms of cost. A comprehensive list is given in Owen (1989).

UNDERSTANDING PROCESS VARIABILITY

CRITICAL KNOWLEDGE FOR MANAGERS

Managers make decisions, often on the interpretation of patterns of variations in data. To do this successfully some knowledge is necessary of the basic statistical concepts needed to interpret variation.

Managers must be able to determine whether the patterns of variation that are observed are indicative of a trend or of random variation similar to that seen in the past. This distinction between patterns of variation is necessary to minimise the losses resulting from misinterpretation of the patterns.

Typical of such losses are:

- blaming people for things they can do nothing about;
- spending money on new equipment that is not needed;
- wasting time looking for explanations of a perceived change when in fact nothing has happened;
- taking action when it would have been better to do nothing.

The concepts of *common* and *special* causes of variation can help to minimise these and other losses.

COMMON AND SPECIAL CAUSES OF VARIATION

A process with only common cause variation is *stable* and is said to be in statistical control. The variation is constant over time. This does not mean that there is no variation, that the variation is small or that it is acceptable to customers (in the above case your boss). A stable process implies only that the variation in the outcomes is predictable within statistically established limits.

A process whose outcomes are affected by both common and special causes is called an *unstable* process. This does not mean that the variation is large, it means that it is unpredictable.

There is another view of variation based upon a classification of process performance as 'good' or 'bad'. This is a very common view but it has several shortcomings. It does not provide any information and it does not therefore provide useful information for improvement. Also, it can lead to fruitless work searching for explanations.

The improvement route is firstly to remove special cause variation so making the process stable, and then to seek to reduce common cause variation.

Continual adjustment of a stable process, that is, one whose output is dominated by common causes, will increase variation and usually make the performance of the process worse. A stable process is most often improved through a fundamental change in the process that reduces or removes some of the common causes.

Many organisations have begun some organised activities to reduce waste and improve efficiency. Generally, these activities begin with much fanfare and commitment by top management to provide resources and training for people in the middle and lower levels to work on problems. These efforts usually produce some improvement during the first year and then level off. There is then frustration on the part of management when progress slows or ceases.

What has usually happened is that initially some special causes have been found and eliminated by common sense and direction of resources. The processes are then dominated by common cause variation and frustration sets in at all levels. Continued progress will require leadership from management to direct activities and make the fundamental changes that will be necessary.

Without some understanding of the ideas underlying variability it will be difficult for managers to provide effective leadership to reduce waste and improve efficiency. Activities include the assignment of people to work on common and special causes. The people appropriate to identify special causes are different from those needed to identify special causes. The same is true of those needed to remove the causes.

We all understand that under everyday conditions things vary. Whether it is the time to answer a telephone, the amount of coffee placed in a cup, the time for a kettle to boil or the wait time for a computer response, variability is a natural fact of existence.

This recognition – that things will never be exactly the same – is important because it allows us to think about and understand the different types of variation that exist in processes.

If we can understand the underlying variability of what we do and start to recognise patterns in that variability then when other causes of variability come along we are better placed to recognise this and take action.

The variation seen in the tally charts and histograms is the combined result of two different types of variation with two different types of cause (for example on page 64).

Common Cause Variation

The first of these is *common cause variation*, also known as *non-assignable* or *chance variation*. Such variation comes from natural causes that occur randomly and are inherent in the process. They cause variation that is outside the control of those carrying out the process. In other words, they are part of the process itself and although they might be reduced they can never be eliminated.

Common cause variation is also predictable and can be planned for. For example, if we know that it takes ten days plus or minus one day to prepare a quotation we can plan for this either by starting earlier or quoting a longer time for the work.

Examples of common cause variation in processes include:

- a process drift due to a backlog;
- differences in working patterns between office teams;
- speed of response of equipment.

Special Cause Variation

Special cause variation, sometimes called *assignable variation*, is the second type of variation and is different in nature. This type has more to do with the way that we choose to operate the process than the process itself. It cannot be planned for, but it can be recognised and acted upon when it occurs to remove it entirely from the system or process.

Special cause variation comes from unpredictable variability due to the way that the process is operated and is generally within the control of either the process owner or process workers. Examples of special causes in service processes include:

- papers lost in transit;
- desks and offices untidy;
- untrained invoice clerks;
- photocopier not maintained;
- systems not available;
- new secretary;
- filing system failing.

Dealing with the Causes of Variation

Generally, management can take action to remove completely the special causes of variation.

If, however, common cause variation is too high and performance figures are unsatisfactory there are only three possible courses of action.

- Improve the process, since the current process cannot perform satisfactorily. For example, if a claims processing process will not meet a target of six days, then we alter the process to meet the target.
- Change the target or specification, since it cannot be met with the current process. As above, though instead we change the target to seven days.
- Suffer the consequences. There is no point shouting at people or disciplining them – the process will not do what is required and it is not their fault.

Two examples illustrate the different types of variation and how they may be dealt with.

Example 1

Suppose that you start work at 8.30 and have on average a 30-minute journey to work. If you leave home at 8.00 every day you will be late approximately half of the time and early half of the time.

Common causes for lateness would include bad weather, red traffic lights or more police cars, all outside your control. Common reasons for being early would include good weather, green traffic lights, fewer police cars – the reverse of the things on the previous list.

You can do nothing about these and although they can be reduced slightly (by leaving at exactly 8.00) they are part of a process called leaving home at 8.00 and driving by the same route to the same place of work.

If told to improve your time-keeping you have few options – change the method of transport, for example to a motor cycle or helicopter; change where you leave from, ie by moving house; leave earlier or change job. All of these change the process itself.

The other real option is to renegotiate your start time or work flexitime to allow more flexibility – changing the requirement or specification.

The only other alternative is to suffer the consequences.

Special causes of variation in journey time would include having to stop for petrol, the alarm not going off or a breakdown. These can be eradicated entirely by filling up the night before, by having two alarm clocks or by ensuring that the car is properly maintained.

In other words, the special causes can be eradicated by action, the common causes minimised. Then if the process still cannot perform we may need a fundamental re-think of the specification.

Example 2

Another example is that of the running of a training course. Suppose that I am running a two-day course. On the first day, two participants were having trouble concentrating. This could be because of a late night or domestic problems. Both of these represent special cause variation.

Now imagine that the whole class is having difficulty. Perhaps the room is too hot, the subject is boring or maybe I am a poor speaker. These are common causes of variation in the concentration of the participants.

The special causes can be eradicated by specific changes – going to bed earlier is one way. To alter the common causes we need to look at the system itself – the materials, the environment or the tutor – as these are having a common effect on all participants.

We can now see a link back to the cause and effect diagram explained in Chapter 6 where the generic causes of variation were the materials, equipment, methods and people carrying out the tasks need to be studied and reasons found for the variation.

Importance of Dealing with Variation Causes in Order

The order in which the two types of variation are dealt with is important. First of all, special causes need to be identified, the root causes found and then these causes eliminated.

When this is done and there are no longer special causes present the process is said to be in statistical control. In other words, the only cause of variation now present is common cause variation. Only when this has been achieved can we go on to examine the common cause variation and look for ways of reducing it.

There are several reasons why this order of events is important. Firstly, special causes of variation may have disproportionate effects on the results found. If invoices routinely take between one and three days to process and one suddenly takes 15 days because it has been lost, this will have a great effect on any statistics produced.

Secondly, what you think are special causes may actually be the beginnings of evidence that two or more processes are being operated at the same time. It can be difficult to work out which is the real process and this problem needs resolution before the process can be analysed and improvements sought.

This approach – removal of special or assignable causes of variation followed by the reduction of common or non-assignable causes of variation – leads us to an overall reduction in variation and so to an improvement in the quality of the process.

ACTION FOLLOWING CONTROL CHART INTERPRETATION

Accurate interpretation of control charts is only part of the application of performance measurement. Once identified, special disturbances must be eliminated if a state of statistical control is to be maintained.

To this end, data collection, charting and interpretation should be conducted as soon as possible after the recorded events; this is to minimise the likelihood of process inputs being lost or forgotten.

Having identified and eliminated special disturbances, a new set of control limits should be calculated based on the next 20 (or so) samples.

Provided the special disturbances were eliminated, the process chart should then indicate a state of statistical control within the recalculated limits. This provides a new base for process monitoring.

The continuing cycle of measurement, monitoring, investigation and action is the practical expression of the never-ending improvement in process efficiency which is the object of statistical process control. This is shown diagrammatically in Figure 10.1.

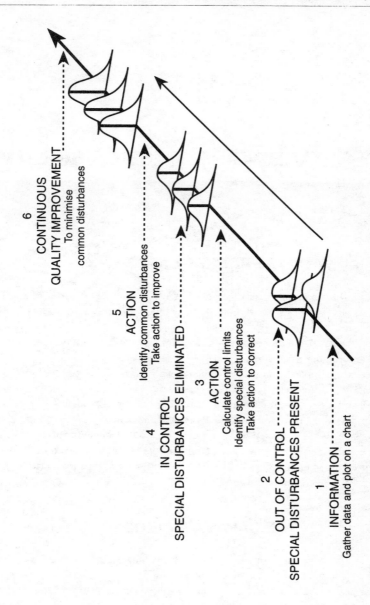

Figure 10.1 *Stages in process improvement.*

11

UNDERSTANDING PROCESS CAPABILITY

WHAT IS PROCESS CAPABILITY?

Chapter 10 on common and special causes of variation discussed the idea of a stable process, one that is within statistical control. Stable processes have known variability that is predictable over time.

However, the fact that a process is stable does not necessarily mean that the output is acceptable or desirable.

Consider, for example, an insurance company with a claims processing process that routinely handles all motor claims within six working days, with all claims being processed between five and seven days. If the company has advertised that all claims will be cleared within eight days then the process is both acceptable and stable; if the marketing claim states that all claims are processed within six days, then it is stable but unacceptable.

The idea that brings together the acceptability of the output from a process (does it meet our specification or target?) with the actual performance of the process (what does it actually do?) is called *process capability*.

THE CAPABILITY INDEX

Process capability is an index or number that tells us how capable our process is and allows the percentage or proportion outside of our target to be calculated.

For example, in the above scenario the marketing claim is that all claims will be processed between five and seven days with a mean value of six days. If this is exactly achieved then the process capability index has a value of 1. If it is bettered (perhaps all claims are processed within five and a half and six and a half days) then the value is greater than 1. If the actual performance is worse than the promise (all claims between five and nine days) then the index is less than 1. In other words, the higher the value of the index the more capable the process.

Because the calculation of the capability index requires a stable process, the process must have no special causes present. In other words, capability only exists if the process is under statistical control.

The reasons for this are twofold. Firstly, the process is not predictable when special causes are present so we cannot be sure over time where the process is going. Secondly, the existence of special cause variation may in fact mean that there is more than one process in operation and that the capability index may be meaningless.

The first step towards the calculation of capability therefore involves the removal of special causes of variation.

Since capability indices tell us what our process is capable of doing, rather than what we are doing to the process, we also need to ensure that for the purposes of the calculation the process is being operated to an optimum level, with the staff well trained and all equipment fully maintained. If these are not the case then we will make the process appear worse than it is.

Variable data from administrative processes is of two types – normally distributed data where the histogram of the data is symmetrical about a central value, and non-normal data where the histogram generally is skew distributed.

Normal data comes from processes such as the measurement of the backlog of documents to be processed or the volume of unprocessed cash at the end of a working day. The histogram of this data will take the shape shown in Figure 11.1.

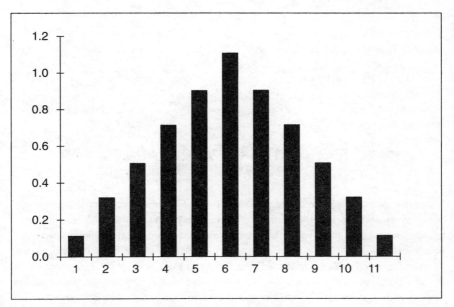

Figure 11.1 *Histogram of normal data for unprocessed cash.*

Non-normal data comes from time-related measures such as the processing time for orders or documents. This is a natural facet of the data, since documents cannot be processed in negative time, and there may be a physical minimum time to carry out the processing, whereas the maximum time may be very large. The histogram of this data will take the shape shown in Figure 11.2.

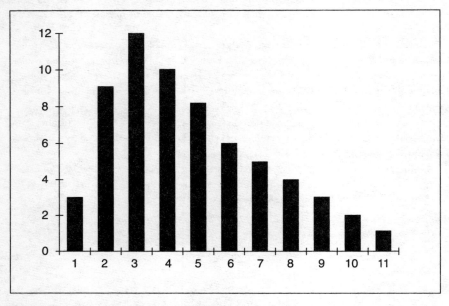

Figure 11.2 *Histogram of non-normal (skewed) data for document processing time.*

CALCULATING THE CAPABILITY INDEX FOR NORMAL DATA

Generally, in service or administrative areas there is only one specification or target value, that is an upper limit on response time or unprocessed cash. If we were seeking to monitor sales figures then there would be a lower limit on a sales manager's figures but not a higher one.

Taking the example of unprocessed cash at the end of a working day, let us assume that we have been monitoring the process and the volume of cash and that we have a control chart drawn on a daily basis. For this example we will use the following figures:

The sample size is 1.	(There is only one reading each day.)
The overall mean $\bar{x}$ is 318.2.	(This is the central line of the x moving range chart.)
The average range $\bar{R}$ is 12.4.	(This is the centre value of the R chart.)
The target value for the maximum amount of unprocessed cash is £340.	(This is the upper specification or target called US.)

We need to estimate the standard deviation of the data from the known range $\bar{R}$. This is done using a statistical constant d_2 using the formula:

$$s = \frac{\bar{R}}{d_2}$$

From Appendix 3, the value of d_2 for $n = 2$ is 1.128. (The capability calculation worksheet at the end of this book give values of d_2 for other values of n.)

The calculation of the capability index C_{pk} is then simply:

$$C_{pk} = \frac{(US - x)}{3 \times s}$$

So: $s = 12.4/1.128 = 10.99$

and:

$$C_{pk} = \frac{(340 - 318.2)}{3 \times 10.99}$$

$$= \frac{21.8}{32.97} = 0.66$$

Since this value is less than 1 the process is incapable. In fact, this is obvious when the target value is drawn on the histogram of the data as in Figure 11.3.

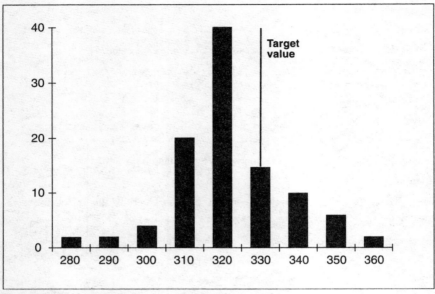

Figure 11.3 *Histogram for unprocessed cash with target value.*

CALCULATING THE CAPABILITY INDEX FOR SKEWED OR NON-NORMAL DATA

In practice most data relating to the time to perform a task and process a document or form is non-normal and is usually skew in form. That is to say, the distribution is of the shape shown in Figure 11.2.

There are several ways of calculating capability for this type of data and some of these involve transformation of the data (often using something called a Weibull transformation which is beyond the scope of this text) and then calculating the capability.

There is a method proposed by John Clements (1989) that uses a set of curves known as the Pearson curves to calculate capability directly. The advantages of this method are:

▩ when the distribution is normal, the indices are the same as given by the above method;
▩ the only difference from the traditional calculation is the method for calculating the size and position of the tails of the distribution;
▩ it can be illustrated using the actual distribution;
▩ no complicated transformation is required;
▩ calculation is easy.

To work the calculation two further statistics are needed.

So far we are familiar with the mean, range and standard deviation of sets of data. There are two other statistics that help to describe the shape of a distribution. These are the *skewness* and *kurtosis*.

Skewness

The skewness of a distribution is a measure of how much to one side or the other of the mean value a distribution lies. A coefficient of skewness C_s is calculated which has the following characteristics:

- It will be zero if the distribution is perfectly symmetrical, in other words a normal distribution has no skewness.
- It will be positive for a distribution with a longer tail on the right (the usual case for data relating to time to process documents).
- It will be negative for a distribution with a longer tail on the left.

These three cases are illustrated in Figure 11.4. The larger the numerical value of the coefficient, the greater the skewness and hence there is less symmetry in the distribution.

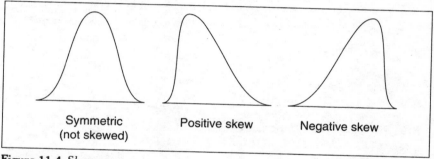

Symmetric Positive skew Negative skew
(not skewed)

Figure 11.4 *Skewness*

From analysis of the data when the mean value is known as $\bar{x}$ and the sample size is n the calculation for C_s is:

$$C_s = \frac{\sqrt{(n \times \sum(x - \bar{x})^3)}}{(\sum(x - \bar{x})^2)^{3/2}}$$

Although seemingly complicated this is easily calculated on computer and is routinely calculated by statistical process control software.

Kurtosis

The kurtosis of a distribution is an indication of how bulging or peaked the distribution is. A coefficient of kurtosis C_k is calculated that has the following characteristics:

- a flat topped distribution will tend to have a low value of C_k;
- a sharp peaked distribution will tend to have a high value of C_k.

A high C_k does not necessarily imply a sharp peak nor a low C_k imply a flat top, because curves with different outlines may have the same value. In fact, C_k is more influenced by the shape of the tails than values near the centre of the distribution.

Two examples of kurtosis are shown in Figure 11.5.

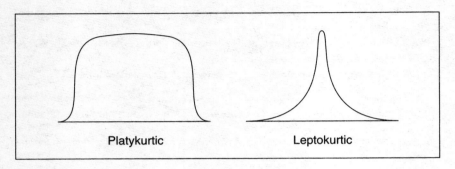

Platykurtic   Leptokurtic

Figure 11.5 *Kurtosis.*

The calculation of C_k is as follows:

$$C_k = \frac{n \times \sum (x - \bar{x})^4}{(\sum (x - \bar{x})^2)^2}$$

Again, this is easily programmed and is usually printed out by statistical process control software.

The Calculation of Capability

The idea behind this calculation is simple. When the data is normally distributed we are comparing the actual process spread between plus and minus three standard deviations with the target or specification. With normal data, 99.73 per cent of all data lies within this range, with 0.135 per cent above the top end and 0.135 per cent below the bottom end.

With normal data these points are symmetrical about the central value and are tabulated and the calculation is straightforward.

With non-normal data it is necessary to calculate directly the points that relate to the plus and minus 0.135 per cent values. This is done using a set of tables – the standardised Pearson curves – shown in the appendices. The calculation is as follows.

Suppose that we have a set of data for times to process invoices. From the data we have calculated the statistics as shown below.

▪ The mean value $\bar{x}$ is 10.2 hours to process the invoice.

- The standard deviation s of the processing time is $s = 2.8$ hours.
- The coefficient of skewness C_s is 1.12.
- The coefficient of kurtosis C_k is 2.62.
- The upper target for processing time U is 20 hours; there is no lower target.
- From the tables we look up the standardised 99.865 per cent value. This is called U_p and the value is 4.736.
- Finally we look up the standardised median (or 50 per cent value). This is called M_p and the value is −0.148.

We first calculate the estimated value U_1 of the upper 99.865 per cent as follows:

$$
\begin{aligned}
U_1 &= \bar{x} + U_p \times s \\
&= 10.2 + (2.8 \times 4.736) \\
&= 13.46
\end{aligned}
$$

The estimated median M, or 50 per cent value is then calculated using the formula

$$
\begin{aligned}
M &= \bar{x} + s \times M_p \\
&= 10.2 + (2.8 \times (-0.148)) \\
&= 9.79
\end{aligned}
$$

The capability index C_{pk} is then calculated as:

$$
\begin{aligned}
C_{pk} &= \frac{(U - M)}{(U_1 - M)} \\
&= \frac{(20 - 9.79)}{(23.46 - 9.79)} \\
&= \frac{10.21}{13.67} \\
&= 0.75
\end{aligned}
$$

In other words, the process in incapable.

Had we done this calculation differently assuming the data was normal the process capability index would have been found to be $C_{pk} = 1.17$ so the skewness of the data leads to very different conclusions about the capability of the process.

The full calculation worksheet can be found in Appendix 7.

IMPLICATIONS OF CAPABILITY

We have targets, the actual performance of the process and a capability index. Suppose now that the calculation has been done and that the process is incapable. There are only three options available.

- Improve the process to improve the capability. Since before calculating capability all the special causes were removed, this means fundamental work on the process itself to make it capable.

■ Change the target value. We know that we cannot meet the existing target consistently and if the process cannot be improved another option is to move the target.

■ Suffer the consequences and deal with problems by firefighting.

All other courses of action will be wasteful of time and effort.

12

MONITORING PROCESSES FOR ERROR

ATTRIBUTE DATA

As well as measuring process performance in terms of, for example, timeliness, using variable data, it is often desirable to monitor processes for error. This is done by using attribute data.

Attribute data are of particular importance in a service or administrative environment when it may not be possible or desirable to take measurements yet there must be some form of performance measurement extracted.

In these cases the improvement of processes comes by way of the reduction of error in the processes progressively to zero. It is likely that attribute data is collected either on a tally chart – for example if we are interested in the number of forms produced that are in error) or a concentration diagram (for example where the type or location of the errors on forms is important and may later be analysed using Pareto analysis). Whatever the method, the flowchart of the process will indicate what and where to measure.

The decision process is the same:

- Draw the flowchart.
- Decide what is important to the process.
- Decide what can go wrong.
- Decide what to measure to tell you if it has gone wrong.
- Agree how to measure it.

The Binomial Distribution

Attribute or counting data allows a specification for accuracy to be set, against which, for example, processes and data or documents produced by processes are tested. There are only two possible answers to this test; they can only be right or wrong – there is no degree of 'rightness'.

This fact makes the definition of the pass/fail criterion particularly important and the uniform application of that criterion essential for the integrity of the data. One widely known example of this type of data is the division of examination marks into grades, where there is not only one pass/fail mark but a series of such marks, by way of which students are allocated examination grades. The decisions made can have major consequences for the futures of the students so it is necessary both to have the division lines between grades correct and the allocation of marks consistently achieved.

A document when checked is either right or wrong and is classed either as defective or not defective. We can then go on to measure and monitor the number of defective documents.

This type of data is from a particular type of distribution known as the *binomial distribution*. According to whether the number of documents examined each time is constant or variable, the type of control chart used to monitor performance is the *np* chart (for when the sample size is constant) or the *p* chart (for when the sample size is variable).

Examples of *np* data are:

▪ defective sales reports when the number of reports daily is constant;
▪ complaints to the sales desk when the daily number of calls is constant;
▪ calls to the help desk when the hourly number is constant.

The way to remember this is that when *np* data is used we are counting the *number* of defective invoices so *n* is for number.

Examples of *p* data are:

▪ defective invoices where the number of invoices inspected daily varies;
▪ defective coding on purchase orders with a varying number of purchase orders;
▪ delivery notes in error when the number of deliveries varies daily;
▪ defective order forms;
▪ incorrectly filled in sales notes.

All are defective items.

Again, this is easily remembered. The *percentage* (or proportion) of defective invoices is being monitored, so *p* is for percentage or proportion.

The Poisson Distribution

Besides the number of defective documents we might also be interested in the number of individual errors or defects within those documents. In other words a defective document may contain one, two, three or more defects or errors. For example, a purchase order may have an incorrect address, customer name and colour of item ordered. This is one defective purchase order with three individual errors. If this is what actually is of interest we would go on to measure and monitor the number of defects or individual errors.

This type of data comes from a particular type of distribution called the *Poisson distribution*. Again, the type of chart used depends on whether the sample size is constant or variable. For a constant or fixed sample size the *c* chart is used, for a variable sample size it is necessary to use a *u* chart. Examples of *c* data are:

- a count of the errors on 100 purchase orders daily;
- the number of individual queries to a help desk in a constant time.

The way to remember this is that we are counting the defects and c is for count.
  Examples of u data are:

- errors on invoices when the number issued varies;
- errors in despatches when the weekly number varies;
- errors on purchase orders;
- errors on sales returns;
- errors on export documents.

In other words – errors or defects. We are now monitoring the number of defects per invoice or per *unit u* and *u* is for errors per unit.

Summary of Types of Attribute Data

The four different types of attribute data are shown in the following table:

	Defects	Defective Units
Constant	c	np
Variable	u	p

For convenience, if the sample size only varies within plus or minus 25 per cent of the average sample size $\bar{n}$ then it may be treated as constant and the average sample size $\bar{n}$ used.

So if the average of all the sample sizes is 100, provided that all the individual sample sizes are between 75 and 125 it is correct to use the average sample size 100 for all the calculations.

Of course, there is far more attribute data in the world than variable data since it is always possible to create attribute data from variable data by setting a specification and then classifying the data as passing or failing that specification. This is what happens, for example, when examination bodies classify individual marks into grades. Pass marks are set between grades and students are classified accordingly.

Conversely, it is usually the case that variable data cannot be created from attribute data since there are no scale values – things are seldom 0.8 right or 0.6 in error.

Using Attribute Data

Three points should be made about the use of attribute data for improvement purposes. The first is that if there are no failures or errors there will be no attribute data. In other words, attribute data depends on the presence of failure. In these circumstances variable data may still exist. This lack of attribute data can make it difficult to bring about improvement, since one route to improvement is via the reduction or removal of error and without error we cannot do this. It is possible to get around this difficulty by introducing tougher internal standards, if appropriate.

Secondly, attribute data can be unstable at small sample sizes. For example, if ten people took an examination and seven passed, the pass rate is seven out of ten or 70 per cent. Suppose now that a further candidate takes the examination and passes. The pass rate is now eight out of eleven or 73 per cent. This is very different from the first result. However, if the figures had been 700 out of 1,000 – still 70 per cent – a change to 701 out of 1,001 would have made little difference.

Attribute data needs a large sample size to become stable. A sample size of 100 is generally recognised as the smallest acceptable for stability.

In the above example, if variable data were being used the addition of one or more additional points would have made very little difference to the stability of the data and the overall picture. It is the absolute pass or fail nature of attribute data that causes the problem.

Finally, the pass/fail criterion can be very important to the actual pass rates, where with variable data the results would have been unaltered. Examples of this can be seen, for example, in examination grades where the exact border between grades can have a major impact on results and people's lives.

Attribute data does, however, provide useful information about the presence of assignable or special cause variation – a preponderance of one failure mode (or error type) usually suggests a systematic failure – so a mixture of variables and attribute data is ideal.

It is possible to be very inventive when creating attribute data. For example, one organisation decided that it was not in the business of making photocopies, so it defined every ream of photocopier paper issued as a failure. They then proceeded to measure and monitor the issue of the paper. As a result of focusing in this way, the usage dropped by more than 35 per cent in the first month and the new, lower, level of use was maintained.

The same organisation defined usage of first-class mail and making outside telephone call before 1 pm as failures and saw similar results. All they had done was define a requirement and then measure a pass or fail against it.

Attribute data also introduces people to data who would normally have found it difficult to think of measurement in their job. Having once seen that they are part of a process that can be measured for error they become more able to think about quality and quality improvement.

DRAWING THE *np* CHART

The *np* chart is used to monitor the number of defective items when the sample size is constant so it could, for example, be used to monitor the number of defective invoices in a daily or weekly sample of 100.

Suppose that examination of the process flowchart of the outline invoicing process for a medium-sized agency operation revealed that the critical point of the process was the allocation of purchase order codes against the department making the purchase.

A quality improvement team was set up to collect data on the number of invoices with incorrect departmental codes. The team used tally charts to collect weekly data on the accuracy or completeness of the invoices.

The example below shows data from this invoicing process. The number sampled each week is 100. The tally chart for the first 13 weeks of the year is given below:

Week number	Number defective
1	~~IIII~~ 11
2	~~IIII~~
3	11
4	~~IIII~~ 1
5	~~IIII~~
6	~~IIII~~
7	~~IIII~~ 111
8	~~IIII~~
9	~~IIII~~ 1
10	~~IIII~~
11	~~IIII~~ 1
12	~~IIII~~ 111
13	1111

The first step in the construction of any attribute chart should always be the compilation of a table showing the complete set of figures. This makes the resulting calculations easier to follow and helps to avoid errors in the calculations.

This data can now be transferred onto a table to form the basis of the np chart as follows:

Week number	Number sampled np	Number defective
1	100	7
2	100	5
3	100	2
4	100	6
5	100	4
6	100	5
7	100	8
8	100	5
9	100	6
10	100	5
11	100	6
12	100	8
13	100	4
Total		71

This is np data for two reasons. Firstly, we are dealing with defective invoices and secondly, the sample size is constant. The name of this data is np. When we come next to draw the p chart the data is of the same type and has the same name.

This data is simply plotted on the np chart as in Figure 12.1. The timescale in weeks is on the horizontal axis, the number of invoices in error on the vertical axis.

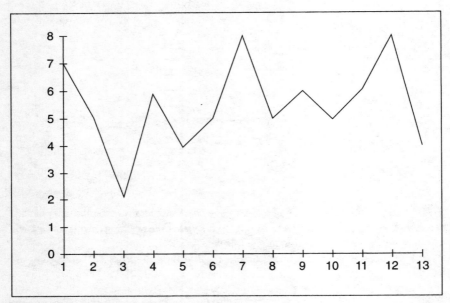

Figure 12.1 *The basic np chart.*

From the data we know that:

The total number of weeks sampled	m =	13
The sample size each week	n =	100

We can calculate the total number of invoices in error

$$\Sigma np = 71$$

The centre line of the np chart is called $\overline{np}$ and is calculated as:

$$\overline{np} = \frac{\Sigma np}{m} = \frac{71}{13} = 5.46$$

This represents the mean value of the number of invoices in error each week.

This centre line is then added to the np chart as shown in Figure 12.2.

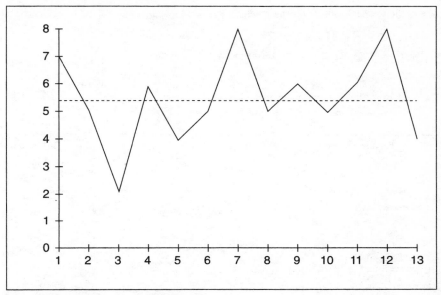

Figure 12.2 *The np chart with centre line.*

Looking at the data this value makes intrinsic common sense. It is the average number of invoices in error each week and passes through the centre of the points on the chart.

We need to calculate the average error in each invoice $\bar{p}$ for later use in the calculation. This is done as follows:

$$\bar{p} = \frac{\overline{np}}{n} = \frac{5.46}{100} = 0.0546$$

Like all the control charts seen previously the np chart has upper and lower control limits about the centre line. Again, these represent plus and minus three standard deviations about the central value $\overline{np}$ and are symmetrical about this value.

As stated previously, np data comes from a particular type of distribution known as the binomial distribution. The formula for three standard deviations is:

$$3 \times \sqrt{(\overline{np})} \times \sqrt{(1-\bar{p})}$$

All of these numbers are known from the earlier calculations so this calculation is simply :

$$3 \times \sqrt{(5.46)} \times \sqrt{(1 - 0.0546)}$$
$$= 3 \times \sqrt{(5.46)} \times \sqrt{(0.9454)}$$
$$= 6.82$$

The upper control limit for the np chart is then:

$$\text{UCL} = \overline{np} - 3 \text{ standard deviations}$$
$$= 5.46 + 6.82$$
$$= 12.28$$

and the lower control limit for the np chart is:

$$LCL_{np} = \overline{np} - 3 \text{ standard deviations}$$
$$= 5.46 - 6.82$$
$$= 0$$

since the lower limit can never be less than zero.

The completed np chart is then drawn as shown in Figure 12.3.

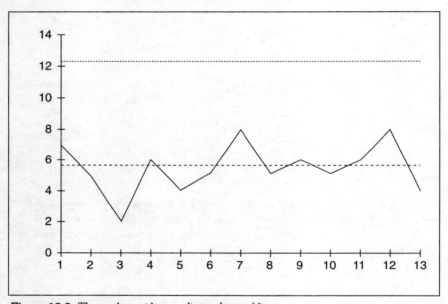

Figure 12.3 *The np chart with centre line and control lines.*

Several simple tips help with the calculations. Firstly, since there can only ever be a complete number of invoices, the centre line of 5.46 can be drawn anywhere between 5 and 6 so drawing the value at 5.5 makes the plotting easier. Secondly, an upper control limit of 12.28 effectively means that 12 represents no change and 13 shows a change has occurred, so for convenience the line can be drawn at 12.5.

One frequent mistake in the calculation lies in the square root of $(1 - \bar{p})$. A check on the calculation can be made from the fact that the square root of a number less than 1 will always be greater than the original number. For example, the square root of 0.81 is 0.9, so the square root of $(1 - \bar{p})$ will always be greater than $\bar{p}$ itself.

It might seem strange to bother with calculating a centre line and a lower control limit, because since the specification is zero defective invoices, surely we are only interested in detecting when things get worse. In fact, the presence of the central line and lower limit helps us detect when the process has actually improved, as well as help in the interpretation of the control chart.

Control Chart Interpretation

Whereas with the variable charts there were always two charts to interpret – the mean and the range – with the *np* chart there is only one chart to be considered.

The rules for interpretation are as follows :

∎ *Are there points outside the upper or lower control limits?* This is a strong indication that the process has gone out of statistical control and is usually a sign that special causes of variation are present.

It is now necessary to examine the process, usually using cause and effect analysis, to find out what has happened, to remove the root cause of the problem and then to bring the process back into statistical control.

Examples of special causes of variation in an invoicing process could be the presence of an untrained invoicing clerk, the introduction of new forms without training or a sticking keyboard on an input computer.

∎ *A run of seven or more points on one side of the central line, either above or below.* Again, the process is out of statistical control and the root cause needs to be found.

The fact that the points could be below the central line might mean that the situation has improved, and if we could find out why and hold the new situation then we will have maintained the improvement.

If the run of points is above the line it means that the performance of the process has changed for the worse, the root cause needs to be determined and eradicated.

Examples here could relate to different work patterns between two teams, differences in the actual invoicing process between two working areas or perhaps the non-availability of control data on one shift.

∎ *A run of eight or more points either increasing or decreasing.* Remember here that the first point in the sequence counts as point zero. The process is out of statistical control.

Clearly, left for long enough, the trend will take the line outside the upper or lower control limits but the rule has given advance warning of what is happening and we need to find out why.

The circumstance here often relates to a backlog of forms to process that is increasing, increasing waiting time for equipment or maintenance overruns on equipment.

Capability Index for *np* Data

The idea of capability with *np* data is analogous to that of capability with variable data.

The specification for the desired number of defective invoices will usually be zero – who aims to produce bad work! The definition of capability is then: 'How many invoices do we expect to produce right first time?'

The calculation is simply:

$$\begin{aligned} \text{Capability} \; &= \; (1-\bar{p}) \times 100\% \\ &= \; (1-0.0546) \times 100\% \\ &= \; 94.54\% \end{aligned}$$

This is sometimes referred to as the first-run or right-first-time capability of the process.

DRAWING THE p CHART

The p chart is used to monitor the number of defective items when the sample size is variable by more than plus or minus 25 per cent of the average sample size, so it could, for example, be used to monitor the number of defective export documents in a month or monthly sample.

Suppose that examination of the process flowchart of the purchase order process for a large service organisation revealed that the critical point of the process was the allocation of purchase order codes against the department making the purchase.

A quality improvement team was set up to collect data on the number of orders with incorrect departmental codes. The team used tally charts to collect monthly data on the accuracy or completeness of the documents. The number sampled each month varied.

As always, the first step in the construction of any attribute chart should be the construction of a table showing the complete set of figures. This makes the resulting calculations easier to follow and helps to avoid errors in those calculations. The data collected for 12 months was as follows:

Month	Number presented	Number of discrepancies np
June	79	58
July	75	41
August	50	27
September	38	15
October	31	14
November	39	18
December	23	13
January	60	40
February	38	16
March	72	37
April	60	32
May	38	20

This is p data for two reasons. Firstly, we are dealing with defective documents and secondly, the sample size is variable. The name of this data is np. When we drew the np chart the data was of the same type and had the same name.

The next step is to calculate the percentages that will be plotted on the p chart. This is done for each of the 12 months as follows.

Month	Number presented	Number of discrepancies np	% in error
June	79	58	73.4
July	75	41	54.7
August	50	27	54.0
September	38	15	39.5
October	31	14	45.2
November	39	18	46.1
December	23	13	56.5
January	60	40	66.7
February	38	16	42.1
March	72	37	51.4
April	60	32	53.3
May	38	20	52.6

This data is simply plotted on the p chart as shown in Figure 12.4. The timescale in months is on the horizontal axis, the percentage of documents in error on the vertical axis.

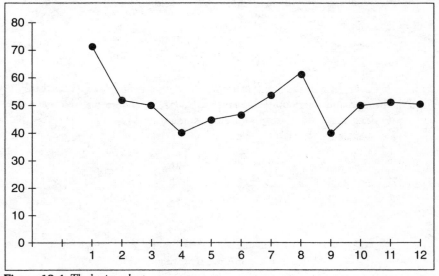

Figure 12.4 *The basic p chart.*

We then go on to calculate the total number sampled and the total number in error by adding together the columns of the table:

Month	Number presented	Number of discrepancies np	% in error
June	79	58	73.4
July	75	41	54.7
August	50	27	54.0
September	38	15	39.5
October	31	14	45.2
November	39	18	46.1
December	23	13	56.5
January	60	40	66.7
February	38	16	42.1
March	72	37	51.4
April	60	32	53.3
May	38	20	52.6
Total	603	331	

From the data we know that:

The total number of months sampled $m = 12$

The total sample size $\Sigma n = 603$

The average sample size $\bar{n}$ can be calculated by:

$$\bar{n} = \frac{\Sigma n}{m} = \frac{603}{12} = 50.25$$

So the rule of plus or minus 25 per cent around the average sample size means that, provided there are sample sizes outside the range 37 to 63, we are dealing with true p data and cannot draw an np chart, using the average sample size $\bar{n}$.

We can calculate the total number of documents in error:

$$\Sigma np = 331$$

The mean value of the p chart is called $\bar{p}$ and is calculated as:

$$\bar{p} = \frac{\Sigma np}{\Sigma n} = \frac{331}{603} = 0.549$$

This represents the mean value of the number of documents in error each week.

The value plotted as the centre line is $\bar{p}$ per cent which is calculated by multiplying $\bar{p}$ by 100:

$$\text{Centre line} = \bar{p} \times 100 = 54.9\%$$

This centre line is then added to the p chart as shown in Figure 12.5

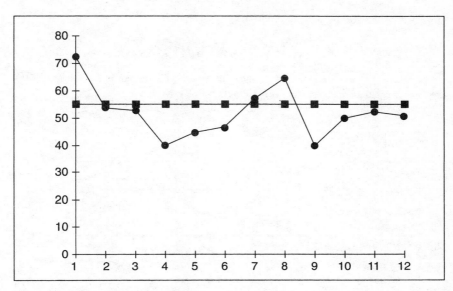

Figure 12.5 *The p chart with centre line.*

Looking at the data this value again makes intrinsic common sense. It is the average number of documents in error each month and passes through the centre of the points on the chart.

Note of course that we cannot add together the different p values and divide by 12, since the bases of the percentages are different and this figure would not be an accurate measure of the mean.

Like all the control charts seen previously the p chart has upper and lower control limits about the centre line. Again, these represent plus and minus three standard deviations about the central value $\bar{p}$ and are symmetrical about this value.

As stated previously, p data comes from a particular type of distribution known as the binomial distribution.

The formula for three standard deviations is:

$$\frac{3 \times \sqrt{(\bar{p})} \times \sqrt{(1-\bar{p})}}{\sqrt{(\bar{n})}}$$

where the value of n varies from month to month.

All of these numbers are known from the earlier calculations so this calculation is simply :

$$\frac{3 \times \sqrt{(0.549)} \times \sqrt{(0.451)}}{\sqrt{(50.25)}} = 0.211$$

The upper control limit for the p chart is then:

$$\text{UCL}_p = \bar{p} + 3 \text{ standard deviations}$$
$$= 0.549 + 0.211 = 0.76$$

and the lower control limit for the p chart is:

$$\text{LCL}_p = \bar{p} - 3 \text{ standard deviations}$$
$$= 0.549 - 0.211 = 0.338$$

These values are translated into percentages immediately before plotting. If the lower control limit is calculated as less than zero then the value is assumed to be zero.

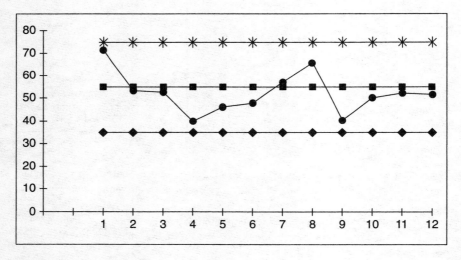

Figure 12.6 *The p chart with centre line and control lines.*

The completed p chart is then drawn as shown in Figure 12.6. Several simple tips help with the calculations. One frequent mistake in the calculation lies in the square root of $(1 - \bar{p})$.

A check on the calculation can be made from the fact that the square root of a number less than 1 will always be greater than the original number. For example, the square root of 0.81 is 0.9, so the square root of $(1 - \bar{p})$ will always be greater than $\bar{p}$ itself.

The second tip is to work in p and $\bar{p}$ until plotting the points and turn these into percentages at the last possible moment. This avoids the possibility of using numbers and percentages in the same calculations. (As an aside, if the resulting numbers seem to make little sense it is likely that this confusion has taken place.)

It might seem strange to bother with calculating a centre line and a lower control limit because, since the specification is zero defective invoices, surely we are only interested in detecting when things get worse. In fact, the presence of the central line and lower limit help us detect when the process has actually improved, as well as help in the interpretation of the control chart.

Indeed, there will only ever be a positive lower control line if the process is behaving very badly. In most real applications the lower limit would be zero.

Control Chart Interpretation

Whereas with the variable charts there were always two charts to interpret – the mean and the range – with the p chart there is only one chart to be considered.

The rules for interpretation are the same as those in page 115.

Capability Index for p Data

The idea of capability with p data is analogous to that of capability with variable data.

The specification for the desired number of defective letters of credit will usually be zero – who aims to produce bad work! The definition of capability is then: 'How many letters of credit do we expect to produce right first time?'

The calculation is simply:

$$\text{Capability} = (1-\bar{p}) \times 100\%$$
$$= (1-0.546) \times 100\%$$
$$= 54.6\%$$

This is sometimes referred to as the first-run or right-first-time capability.

DRAWING THE c CHART

The c chart is used to monitor the number of defects produced when the sample size is constant or variable by less than plus or minus 25 per cent of the average sample size, so it could, for example, be used to monitor the number of errors found during a complete stocktake or the number of mistakes on sales order forms.

Suppose that examination of the process flowchart of the outline stocktaking process for a large service organisation revealed that the critical point of the process was the accurate recording of all relevant data during the stock count. At this point a manual system is used and either missing or inaccurate data is critical for both record purposes and the successful fulfilling of future orders.

A quality improvement team was set up to collect data on the number of records with missing or inaccurate data. The team used concentration diagrams to collect weekly data on the accuracy or completeness of the documents and also on the locations in the warehouse where the errors occurred. The number sampled each week was constant.

Again, the first step in the construction of any attribute chart should always be the construction of a table showing the complete set of figures. This makes the resulting calculations easier to follow and helps to avoid errors in those calculations. The data collected for 12 weeks was as follows:

Week no.	Stock counts	Errors c
1	90	++++
2	90	11
3	90	1111
4	90	++++ 11
5	90	++++ 1
6	90	++++
7	90	11
8	90	11
9	90	++++ 11
10	90	1111
11	90	11
12	90	111

This data can now be transferred onto a table to form the basis of the c chart.

Week no.	Stock counts c	Errors
1	90	5
2	90	2
3	90	4
4	90	7
5	90	6
6	90	5
7	90	2
8	90	2
9	90	7
10	90	4
11	90	2
12	90	3
Total		49

This is c data for two reasons. Firstly, we are dealing with errors on forms and secondly, the sample size is constant. The name of this data is c. When drawing the u chart the data is of the same type and has the same name.

This data is simply plotted on the c chart as shown in Figure 12.7. The timescale in weeks is on the horizontal axis, the number of errors per form on the vertical axis.

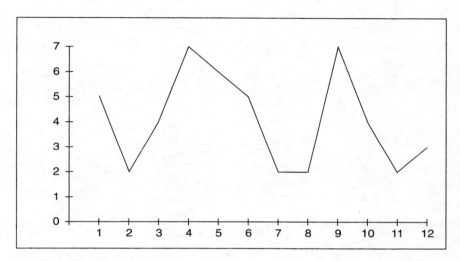

Figure 12.7 *The basic c chart.*

From the data we know that:

The total number of weeks sampled m = 12
The sample size n = 90
The total number of errors Σc = 49

The centre line of the c chart is called $\bar{c}$ and is calculated as:

$$\bar{c} = \frac{\Sigma c}{m} = 4.03$$

This represents the mean value of the number of errors each week. The meaning of 4.03, since there can only ever be a whole number of errors, is that 4 errors or less are below the mean, five or more are above the mean. We can therefore draw the line at 4.5 errors per week.

This centre line is then added to the c chart as shown in Figure 12.8.

Looking at the data this value again makes intrinsic common sense. It is the average number of errors each week on the forms and passes through the centre of the points on the c chart.

Like all the control charts seen previously the c chart has upper and lower control limits about the centre line. Again, these represent plus and minus three standard deviations about the central value $\bar{c}$ and are symmetrical about this value.

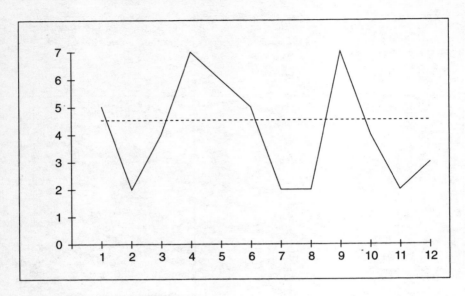

Figure 12.8 *The c chart with centre line.*

As stated previously, c data comes from a particular type of distribution known as the Poisson distribution. The formula for three standard deviations is:

$$3 \text{ standard deviations} = 3 \times \sqrt{(\bar{c})}$$

All of these numbers are known from the earlier calculations so this calculation is simply :

$$= 3 \times \sqrt{(4.03)}$$
$$= 6.06$$

The upper control limit for the c chart is then:

$$\text{UCL}_c = \bar{c} + 3 \text{ standard deviations}$$
$$= 4.03 + 6.06 = 10.09$$

so we plot 10.5 for convenience since in practice 10.09 means 'more than 10 and less than 11'.

And the lower control limit for the c chart is:

$$\text{LCL}_c = \bar{c} - 3 \text{ standard deviations}$$
$$= 4.03 - 6.06 = 0$$

since there can never be a negative number of errors.

The completed c chart is then drawn as shown in Figure 12.9.

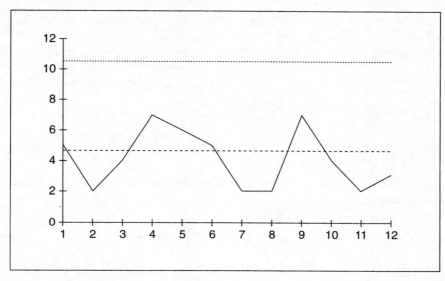

Figure 12.9 *The c chart with centre line and control lines.*

As before, it might seem strange to bother with calculating a centre line and a lower control limit because, since the specification is zero errors, surely we are only interested in detecting when things get worse. In fact, the presence of the central line and lower limit help us detect when the process has actually improved, as well as help in the interpretation of the control chart.

Control Chart Interpretation

Whereas with the variable charts there were always two charts to interpret – the mean and the range – with the c chart there is only one chart to be considered.

The rules for interpretation are the same as those on page 115.

Capability Index for *c* Data

The idea of capability with c data is analogous to that of capability np or p data.

The specification for the desired number of errors will usually be zero – after all, who aims to produce bad work! The definition of capability is then: 'How many documents do we expect to produce error-free first time?'

We know that the average number of defects per unit is [u bar], so we can use the formula for the Poisson distribution to give the likelihood of zero defects:

$$Y = e^{-d/u}$$

where d/u is the average number of errors per unit to calculate the possibility that the work will be error-free.

The calculation is:

Average number of
errors per unit
$$= 4.03/90$$
$$= 0.0448$$

Likelihood of zero defects $= e^{-0.0448}$
$$= 0.956$$
$$= 95.6\%$$

This is sometimes referred to as the first-run or right-first-time capability. It is also called the probability of zero defects.

DRAWING THE u CHART

The u chart is used to monitor the number of defects produced when the sample size is variable by more than plus or minus 25 per cent of the average sample size, so it could, for example, be used to monitor the number of errors found during an audit or the number of mistakes on sales order forms.

Suppose that examination of the process flowchart for the sales order process of a large service organisation revealed that the critical point of the process was the capture of all relevant data during the telephone call. At this point a screen-based form is used and missing or inaccurate data is critical for the successful processing of the order.

A quality improvement team was set up to collect data on the number of screens with missing or inaccurate data The team used concentration diagrams to collect weekly data on the accuracy or completeness of the documents. The number sampled each week varied.

Once again the first step in the construction of any attribute chart should always be the construction of a table showing the complete set of figures. This makes the resulting calculations easier to follow and helps to avoid errors in those calculations. The data collected for 12 weeks was transferred onto a table to form the basis of the u chart:

Week	Calls n	Errors c
1	700	20
2	800	130
3	700	30
4	700	100
5	800	70
6	600	60
7	800	140
8	600	20
9	400	10
10	300	60
11	400	40
12	400	20

This is u data for two reasons. Firstly, we are dealing with errors on documents and secondly, the sample size is variable. The name of this data is c. When we drew the c chart the data was of the same type and had the same name.

It is obvious from the type of data that since each call can have more than one error it is possible for the number of errors per call to be greater than one.

The next stage is to calculate the number of errors or defects per document or u. This is the statistic that will be plotted on the control chart.

Week	Calls n	Errors c	Errors per call $u = c/n$
1	700	20	0.029
2	800	130	0.163
3	700	30	0.043
4	700	100	0.143
5	800	70	0.088
6	600	60	0.100
7	800	140	0.180
8	600	20	0.033
9	400	10	0.025
10	300	60	0.200
11	400	40	0.100
12	400	20	0.050
Total	7,200	700	

The total number of calls Σn and the total number of errors Σc are also shown.

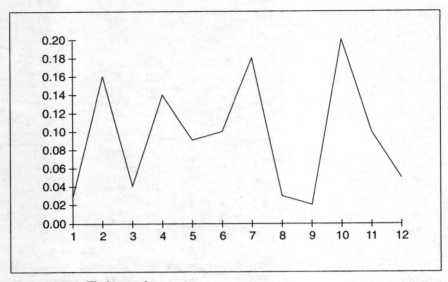

Figure 12.10 *The basic u chart.*

This data is simply plotted on the u chart as shown in Figure 12.10. The timescale in weeks is on the horizontal axis, the number of errors per document on the vertical axis.

From the data we know that:

The total number of weeks sampled $\quad m = 12$

The total sample size $\qquad\qquad \Sigma n = 7{,}200$

The average sample size $\bar{n} \qquad = \dfrac{\Sigma n}{m} = \dfrac{7{,}200}{12}$

$$= 600$$

The total number of errors $\qquad \Sigma c = 700$

The centre line of the u chart is called $\bar{u}$ and is calculated as:

$$\bar{u} = \frac{\Sigma c}{\Sigma n} = \frac{700}{7{,}200} = 0.097$$

This represents the mean value of the number of errors each week.

This centre line is then added to the u chart as shown in Figure 12.11.

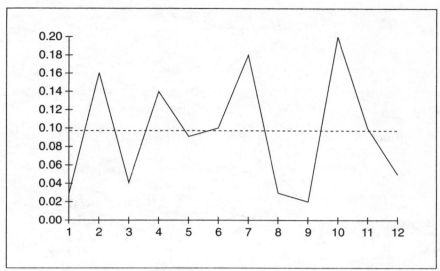

Figure 12.11 *The u chart with centre line*

Looking at the data this value again makes intrinsic common sense. It is the average number of errors each week and passes through the centre of the points on the u chart.

Like all the control charts seen previously the u chart has upper and lower control limits about the centre line. Again, these represent plus and minus three standard deviations about the central value $\bar{u}$ and are symmetrical about this value.

As stated previously, u data comes from a particular type of distribution known as the Poisson distribution. The formula for three standard deviations is:

$$3 \text{ standard deviations} \quad = \frac{3 \times \sqrt{u}}{\sqrt{(n)}}$$

All of these numbers are known from the earlier calculations so this calculation is simply :

$$
\begin{aligned}
3 \text{ standard deviations} \quad &= \frac{3 \times \sqrt{(0.097)}}{\sqrt{(600)}} \\
&= 3 \times 0.0127 \\
&= 0.038
\end{aligned}
$$

The upper control limit for the u chart is then:

$$
\begin{aligned}
UCL_u &= \bar{u} + 3 \text{ standard deviations} \\
&= 0.097 + 0.038 \\
&= 0.135
\end{aligned}
$$

and the lower control limit for the u chart is:

$$\begin{aligned} \mathrm{LCL}_u &= \bar{u} - 3 \text{ standard deviations} \\ &= 0.097 - 0.038 \\ &= 0.059 \end{aligned}$$

The completed u chart is then drawn as shown in Figure 12.12.

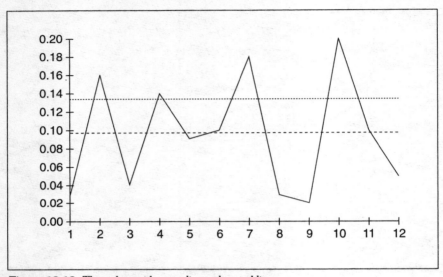

Figure 12.12 *The u chart with centre line and control lines.*

It might seem strange to bother with calculating a centre line and a lower control limit because, since the specification is zero errors, surely we are only interested in detecting when things get worse. In fact, the presence of the central line and lower limit help us detect when the process has actually improved, as well as help in the interpretation of the control chart.

Control Chart Interpretation

Whereas with the variable charts there were always two charts to interpret – the mean and the range – with the u chart there is only one chart to be considered.

The rules for interpretation are the same as those on page 115.

Capability Index for *u* Data

The idea of capability with u data is analogous to that of capability with other attribute data such as p, np or c data.

The specification for the desired number of errors in documents will usually be zero, since the target for error is usually zero. The definition of capability is then: 'How many documents do we expect to produce error-free first time?'

We know that the average number of defects per unit is $\bar{u}$, so we can use the formula for the likelihood of zero defects:

$$Y = e^{-d/u}$$

to calculate the possibility that the work will be error-free.

The calculation is:

$$\text{Likelihood of zero defects} = e^{-0.097}$$
$$= 0.91$$

This is sometimes referred to as the first-run or right-first-time capability. It is also called the probability of zero defects.

ATTRIBUTE DATA CONTROL CHARTS – SUMMARY

Proportion Defective (p) Charts

The p chart is used for process control when there is variation in successive sample sizes and when the available information is of the fraction or proportion of defectives in a sample. The same control lines can be used when sample sizes do not vary by more than 25 per cent, ie new control lines must be calculated for samples that vary by more than 25 per cent.

Number Defective (np) Charts

np charts are similar to p charts, the difference being that sample sizes must be constant because the actual number of defectives is plotted. Tables are available that remove the need for calculation of np chart control limits.

Number of Defects (c) Charts

The c chart is similar to the p chart except that the sample size must be constant and it describes defects not defectives. The samples might be single units or constant sized groups of units, eg

▦ the number of errors on sales order forms;
▦ a constant sized group of samples such as a fixed-quantity inspection, eg a daily audit of ten similar forms from the previous day where the total number of faults is recorded.

Number of Defects per Unit (*u*) Charts

The *u* chart is similar to the *c* chart, except that the mean number of defects per sample is calculated and recorded. It is used when the sample size varies, provided the sample to sample variation is not more than 25 per cent, eg the number of errors in a computer program.

13

DETECTING PROCESS CHANGES USING CUSUMS

INTRODUCTION TO CUSUMS

Control charts are designed to look at a process and detect whether it has changed or gone out of statistical control. They take data and plot it against time, adding a centre line and upper and lower control limits. The main use is for real-time control of the process. The basis is the taking of a sample, calculation, plotting the points, interpretation and then action.

Cumulative *sums*, or cusums, are another way to analyse process performance and detect changes.

There are other uses of cusums that allow historical data to be examined to reveal possible cause and effect relationships, for example between the success of a particular training course (the cause) and the resultant change in office productivity (the effect).

Cusums can allow large amounts of data to be averaged to reveal long-term changes in performance when the short-term variation may mask the longer-term effects.

By means of the cusum technique it is possible to look back at the data recorded for recent productivity figures and to decide:

■ *if* changes have taken place; and
■ roughly *when* the changes occurred.

CONSTRUCTING A CUSUM CHART

We draw a cusum by collecting the data, which can be in any form. The examples below relate to office productivity figures in percentages and to invoicing errors, but cusums can be used to monitor np data for the number of defective items, p data for the percentage of defective items, u data for defects per unit or c data for the simple count of defects.

The next stage is to identify a constant value against which the values will be measured. This value can be either the historical mean value, the target value or perhaps some specification. We will call this value T.

The advantage of using the historical mean value is that the cusum will start and finish on the horizontal axis. If a value that is too high is chosen the cusum will fall through the floor of the graph; if the value is too small it will go through the roof.

We then take this value away from each successive x_i value to form a residual value $(x_i - T)$.

The next stage is to successively cumulate these $(x_i - T)$ values to form the so-called cumulated residuals. So the first cumulated residual value is $x_1 - T$, the second is $x_1 - T + x_2 - T$, or $x_1 + x_2 - 2T$, etc.

The cumulated residuals are then plotted on the vertical axis against the timescale on the horizontal axis.

Cusums are different from the more usual type of control chart or Shewart chart and interpreting them is also different. This is demonstrated in the following two ways:

■ The slope of the line drawn measures the mean value. Thinking about this it is obvious. Suppose that we are subtracting a constant value of 10 and the current mean level is 11. The residual value will be 1 and the cusum will increase by that constant amount each time a value is added. Equally, if the current mean level is 9 then the residual values will be –1 and the cusum will decrease by that constant amount. We can therefore draw a 'fan' shape that shows the different mean values.

■ A change in the slope indicates a change in the mean value. It is by looking for significant changes in slope that we detect changes in the value being monitored.

Using this information we can draw what is called a *cusum protractor* to show in simple terms what the different slopes mean. This looks like a fan shape and, using the example above, would exhibit different slopes for the different mean values of 9, 10 and 11 as shown in Figure 13.1.

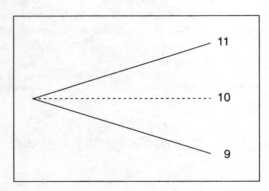

Figure 13.1 *Cusum protractor.*

Examples of the Construction of a Cusum Chart

The technique will be illustrated by the example of an insurance claims processing system. Suppose there was concern over the stagnant levels of productivity in the claims processing office and training courses were identified to change the situation.

Historical levels of productivity were known for each individual in the department and the decision was taken to plot cusums on individual performance before and after the training.

The data for one individual before and after the course is as follows :

Week no.	Productivity %
1	57
2	69
3	64
4	54
5	52
6	76
7	71
8	51
9	53
10	69
11	71
12	61
13	55
14	80
15	81
16	64
17	71
18	58
19	63
20	76
21	95
22	65

From historic data the average productivity level in the past had been 62 per cent. This average level was set as the target for the cusum and the residuals from the new levels calculated as follows:

Week no.	Productivity %	Residual %
1	57	–5
2	69	7
3	64	2
4	54	–8
5	52	–10
6	76	14
7	71	9
8	51	–11
9	53	–9
10	69	7
11	71	9
12	61	–1
13	55	–7
14	80	18
15	81	19
16	64	2
17	7	9
18	58	–4
19	63	1
20	76	14
21	95	33
22	65	3

The cusum values are then created by accumulating the residual values, as follows:

Week no.	Productivity %	Residual %	Cumulated residual
1	57	–5	–5
2	69	7	2
3	64	2	4
4	54	–8	–4
5	52	–10	–14
6	76	14	0
7	71	9	9
8	51	–11	–2
9	53	–9	–11
10	69	7	–4
11	71	9	5
12	61	–1	4
13	55	–7	–3

14	80	18	15
15	81	19	34
16	64	2	36
17	71	9	45
18	58	−4	41
19	63	1	42
20	76	14	56
21	95	33	89
22	65	3	92

The next step is to draw the cusum as shown in Figure 13.2. The horizontal scale is the week number, the vertical scale is the cumulated residual values.

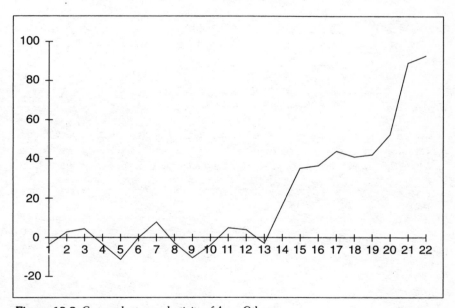

Figure 13.2 *Cusum chart – productivity of Anne Other.*

The cusum protractor is then added as shown in Figure 13.3. Since the target value was 62 per cent, the horizontal line corresponds to 62 per cent, the lines for 72 per cent and 67 per cent are also shown.

The final stage is to interpret the chart. The major change of slope on the chart occurred following week 13. It can be seen that prior to that point the mean value varied about 62 per cent; following week 13 the mean value was about 72 per cent

Looking back, the training had taken place on week 13 and the result of the successful course can be seen in the cusum chart.

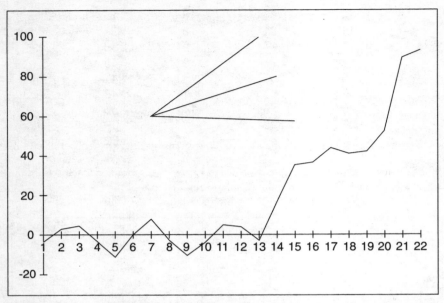

Figure 13.3 *Cusum chart – productivity of Anne Other with protractor.*

We can go one stage further and draw what is called the 'Manhattan diagram' for this data as shown in Figure 13.4. The Manhattan diagram, so called because the shape resembles the skyline of Manhattan, shows the changes in mean level in more conventional form.

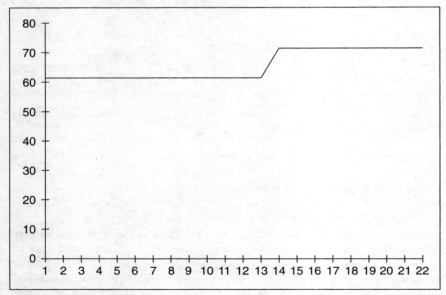

Figure 13.4 *The Manhattan diagram.*

THE DOUBLE CUSUM

In the above application of the cusum the horizontal scale corresponded to time and was fixed. In the example the scale was weeks.

However, it sometimes happens that it is more appropriate to incorporate actual variation of the 'timescale' with the horizontal plotting of the cusum points. This occurs when the sampling varies in terms of the sample size. The resulting plot is known as a *double cusum*.

The following example uses data from an invoicing process. The number of invoices sampled each day varies and data for the first 13 weeks of the year is as follows:

Week number	Number sampled	Number defective
1	23	7
2	15	2
3	31	6
4	12	1
5	33	6
6	28	5
7	12	7
8	18	0
9	22	3
10	41	5
11	35	7
12	31	6
13	38	6
Total	339	61

A standard cusum could be made of the data using the number of error-free invoices against day number. Such an approach would be misleading because of the number of different invoices examined each day.

In this context we are more interested in the proportion of the total number of invoices that have errors rather than in the actual number. Using the above data we can estimate the average number of invoices with errors as:

$$61/339 = 0.1799$$

ie 17.9 per cent of invoices are in error. For convenience this will be rounded to 18.0 per cent or 0.18.

The first step is to calculate the individual values in the table, as follows:

Day number	Number sampled	Number defective	Defective proportion
1	23	7	0.33
2	15	2	0.133
3	31	6	0.194
4	12	1	0.083
5	33	6	0.182
6	28	5	0.179
7	12	7	0.583
8	18	0	0.0
9	22	3	0.136
10	41	5	0.122
11	35	7	0.20
12	31	6	0.194
13	38	6	0.158
Total	339	61	

The figures for the defective proportion of invoices could simply have been used to construct a cusum, but the wide differences in the sample size mean that the resulting chart would have been misleading. This problem is overcome using the double cusum by taking into account the different sample sizes.

We can work out for each day how many invoices would have been expected to be wrong. This is done using the average figure 0.18 together with the sample size each day. For each day we can calculate the difference between the number expected and the actual number found as follows.

▪ *Day 1:* 23 invoices were sampled so the expected number of errors is 23 x 0.18 = 4.14.

Since we actually found 7, this deviates from the expected number by 7 − 4.14 = 2.86 so the residual value is 2.86.

▪ *Day 2:* 15 invoices were sampled so the expected number of errors is 15 x 0.18 = 2.7.

The actual number was 2 so the cusum entry is 2 − 2.7 = −0.7.

The complete cusum table then is as follows:

Day number	Number sampled	Number defective	Defective proportion	Residual
1	23	7	0.33	2.86
2	15	2	0.133	−0.7
3	31	6	0.194	0.42
4	12	1	0.083	−1.16
5	33	6	0.182	0.94
6	28	5	0.179	0.04
7	12	7	0.583	4.84
8	18	0	0.0	−2.34
9	22	3	0.136	0.96
10	41	5	0.122	−2.38
11	35	7	0.20	0.70
12	31	6	0.194	0.42
13	38	6	0.158	0.84
Total	339	61		

The accumulated residuals can then be calculated as before:

Day number	Number sampled	Number defective	Defective proportion	Residual	Cumulative Residual
1	23	7	0.33	2.86	2.86
2	15	2	0.133	−0.7	2.16
3	31	6	0.194	0.42	2.58
4	12	1	0.083	−1.16	1.42
5	33	6	0.182	0.94	2.36
6	28	5	0.179	0.04	2.40
7	12	7	0.583	4.84	7.24
8	18	0	0.0	−2.34	4.90
9	22	3	0.136	0.96	5.86
10	41	5	0.122	−2.38	3.48
11	35	7	0.20	0.70	4.18
12	31	6	0.194	0.42	4.60
13	38	6	0.158	0.84	5.44
Total	339	61			

The cumulated residuals are then plotted as in Figure 13.5 to show the full double cusum.

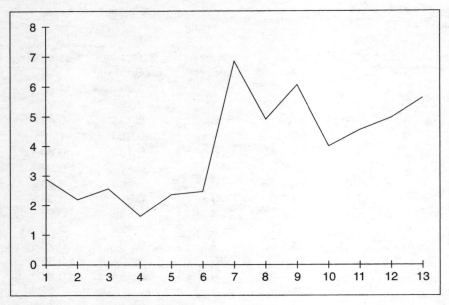

Figure 13.5 *The double cusum chart.*

SUMMARY

Cusums show changes more quickly than the more usual control charts. As a result of this additional sensitivity they can occasionally show changes that are not real and care must be taken in their use. They are more difficult to explain to people used to plotting and interpreting the Shewart charts but the benefit comes from the ability to pinpoint change and relate that change to events.

Cusums also are an excellent way of averaging data to remove short-term fluctuations, so revealing longer-term changes.

14

SELF-MEASUREMENT

Sometimes understanding where you fit in an organisation, how your work contributes to the success of the whole and how to measure your own success can be difficult.

It is generally recognised that the elements that contribute to a job being done well are that the job holder:

- knows what to do – this means being clear about *what* the job is, to *what standards* it should be performed and *how* it fits into the whole process. Having a knowledge of the process flowchart is therefore essential;
- knows how to do it, and therefore has the skills and continuous training necessary;
- has the necessary equipment and materials and any other resources that are needed to do the job;
- can measure performance in terms of the standard of the work that they do, which implies being able to measure and interpret the measurements;
- is able to take corrective action when things go wrong and when and whom they should call for help.

Central to this is measurement.

There are many jobs where measurement appears difficult, yet where simple measures can help people to see how well they are doing, tell them when things are going wrong and pinpoint the areas for improvement. Getting people to measure their own performance can be difficult and in an organisation whose culture centres on blame it is probably not a good idea, but for others it can provide a valuable impetus for improvement.

The self-measurement chart as shown in Figure 14.1 provides a simple mechanism for individuals or groups to measure the effectiveness of their part of a process and identify when things are going wrong.

How to use the measurement chart:

- Define precisely what is to be measured and title the chart. Remember to include in the title the definition of both the error (or non-conformance) to be measured and the activity rate, eg the number of meetings for which you are late out of the total number of meetings attended.

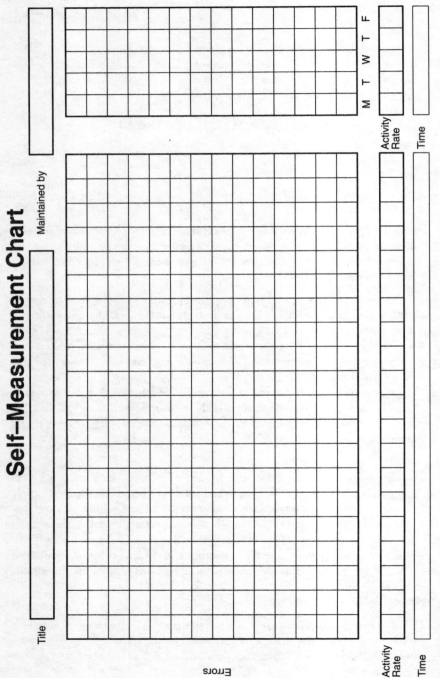

Figure 14.1 *The self-measurement chart.*

■ Use the precise definition of the error as the label for the vertical axis.

■ Decide who will be responsible for updating the chart and put their name on the chart. Place the chart for maximum visibility.

■ Identify how the errors will be counted, who will count them and what time collection interval is most appropriate. If daily collection is appropriate, record both the total number of times you use the process being measured (activity rate) and the total number of errors on the smaller right-hand chart. At the end of each week, sum the activity and the errors and make one entry on the main, left-hand chart. Clear the right-hand chart ready to record the next week's data.

■ Take corrective action and monitor the resulting improvement on the larger chart.

The most practical way to achieve this is to cover the chart with a clear plastic sheet to assist erasure.

Self-measurement charts essentially record errors, problems or some kind of failing to conform to a requirement. The data being generated is therefore attribute data and the data type will be np, p, u or c depending on whether defects or defective items are being measured.

Measurement charts can therefore be taken a stage further and the data plotted on the appropriate attribute chart if so desired.

Measuring quality of work allows explicit demonstration of progress towards improvement. Making data very visible to all employees can also be a great motivator as it helps people to feel in control of the quality of their work, thereby restoring pride as they see how their efforts contribute to the whole.

15

WHY PERFORMANCE MEASUREMENT FAILS

There are a number of assumptions which underline our reluctance to understand more systematically the performance of processes for which we are responsible.

'It's Not For Me'

'It's for my people, not for me. We are very busy. We feel that we do not have the time for statistical details.' Yet it is we who most need the details since the initiation of the improvement is in our hands and we cannot change company systems intelligently without statistical thinking. Competitors in Japan and elsewhere do understand statistical thinking – they should do because they have been applying the concepts for the last 30 years. This is one of the keys to Japanese success.

'It's For Manufacturing'

'It's for manufacturing, not for me.' This is a similar attitude to the previous problem. It is not hard to see why many non-manufacturing people feel this way because of the lack of examples of application in non-manufacturing areas.

The use of statistical techniques in staff areas can lead to much improved control and understanding of processes, though it may be true that the determination of what is to be measured and recorded and the best techniques to use, can be less obvious than in manufacturing.

FALSE STARTS

Management is paid to make decisions which affect the future. More effective decisions can be made on a process which is in statistical control. A process in statistical control will have essentially the same shape, location and spread over time. However, in practice, a process is seldom in statistical control when first investigated.

The first objective of process improvement is to eliminate the special disturbances, leaving only the random variation of a stable process.

A process may change because of moving means or it may change because of moving variability. In practice, we see a combination of these two types of change, and unless we use control charts, we will never see these changes.

There is no substitute for managing our own processes with these techniques to gain a better understanding of their effectiveness. The following 'false start' situations should make more sense for those who have had a chance to use control charts.

▪ Charting a characteristic at a stage in the process where we couldn't really take action on a special disturbance. The stage is typically too far downstream in a process to do any real good because the cause of an out of control signal could be one of many possibilities.

▪ Not reacting to signals of special disturbances because of production pressures.

▪ Not reacting to signals of special disturbances because we are not making any out-of-specification parts at present.

▪ Not reacting to signals of special disturbances because there is no action plan to guide the manager.

▪ Not reacting to signals of special disturbances because control limits are not based on data. Instead, they are based on a percentage of the specifications or arbitrarily based on experience. The result is either over-control or under-control.

▪ Not reacting to signals of special disturbances because the control limits have not been recalculated when they should have been, eg following permanent improvement action on the process.

▪ Not reacting to signals of special disturbances (specifically runs above or below the centre line) because there is no centre line plotted.

▪ A practice of 'punishing the bearer of bad news', so people do anything to keep the process *apparently* in control. Examples are sampling when a 'good' part comes along, poor sampling plans, using modified control limits and other such devices. These tactics keep management in happy ignorance.

▪ Total dependence on an SPC facilitator when quality should be the responsibility of those involved in the process. It is very easy and convenient to rely on a facilitator.

▪ Lack of traceability of data (failure to maintain logs or records of events) which might lead to failure to identify out-of-control signals.

A STRUCTURE FOR IMPROVEMENT

To take root properly in any organisation, performance improvement needs a structure that will define responsibilities and provide the support to ensure that they are met.

In the early stages there will need to be a part-time performance improvement coordinator or manager whose role will be to coordinate the activities across the organisation. For maximum effect the appointment should be at board level and the responsibilities should include:

▪ coordinating the improvement process;
▪ managing and allocating budgets to teams;

- reporting to the steering group on progress;
- calling steering group meetings;
- championing the cause.

A steering group has just been mentioned. This is necessary to manage and legitimise involvement in quality improvement. This steering group is ideally at a level where any conflicts between departments can be resolved.

Part of the purpose of this is to move away from the 'I've done my project' mentality when there have been one or two successes on the road to the idea of continuous improvement, and then things stop.

The steering group should use a performance improvement plan to schedule successive improvement activities that arise from the identification of processes (from the critical success factors and key and sub-processes), from the cost of quality and from the identification of internal customer requirements.

The steering group then authorises the setting up of improvement teams which use the quality improvement process and improvement tools described later in this chapter and then work on the process to bring about improvement.

It is important to recognise that these improvement teams are set up to understand and improve a specific process allocated by the steering group. When they have completed this task they then disband. In other words, they are not some form of quality circle – they are a team set up by the steering group with one purpose.

In contrast, the steering group is a permanent feature of the structure of the organisation. This group has several important aims:

- to manage the overall process;
- to identify improvement opportunities;
- to allocate people to improvement teams;
- to allow people to become involved in the team activity;
- to manage any barriers to improvement;
- to allocate budgets to teams;
- to recognise the success of teams;
- to act as a role model in team behaviour;
- to manage the overall communication surrounding the process.

The overall purpose of the steering group is to demonstrate commitment to the improvement process and to manage it.

The success of the process improvement activities depend very largely on the commitment of those at the top of the organisation and on the support that they give to the process. It is generally recognised that there are three specific components that together lead to success:

- the commitment and leadership shown at the top of the organisation;
- the quality of the improvement planning and the way that it is followed through;
- the training given to those to be involved in improvement activities.

These are like the three legs of a stool. All three together make the stool stand up. Remove any or reduce their effectiveness and the stability of the stool suffers.

Organisations that organise in this way make their success much more likely and deserve the success that they achieve.

A SIMPLE PROCESS FOR PROBLEM-SOLVING

Asking people to work in teams appears deceptively simple – what can be more obvious than getting people to work together to solve problems?

By bringing people together in improvement teams to tackle problems, two difficulties are often immediately created. First, people do not necessarily know how to work together as part of a team. Second, they may lack the necessary technical skills to tackle the problems.

When people understand the 'what' they then need to understand the 'how'. By linking the mission via the critical success factors to the core key processes and sub-processes there may have been created a climate where the hearts and minds have been won over and people have a genuine desire to bring about improvement.

At that stage people can see how what they do contributes to the overall success of the organisation and how they can play a role in improving that success. They can also see that they do not just 'do a job' but that that job has internal customers, people downstream in the process who rely on them to produce good quality work.

This helps to give them a desire to do better – to bring about improvement – but the simple desire is not enough. Having the wish to change without the means can be frustrating and lead to people being disillusioned.

It is important at this stage that people have access to the necessary improvement tools and a process for using them, otherwise there is a risk that people who have been turned on can be as easily turned off if they cannot see a way to turn the desire to improve into action.

The problem-solving process outlined here shows how the tools and techniques described elsewhere in this book along with others can fit together to comprise a powerful toolkit for improvement through teamwork.

The tools and techniques are the simple 'hows' that provide the necessary basic skills for problem-solving. Therefore the problem-solving process says 'finding root cause' and the tools say 'cause and effect analysis'.

The Problem-solving Process

The problem-solving process is a logical sequence for solving problems and improving the quality of decisions. It is also a guide to identifying which tools and techniques to apply. It can be applied to any problem or deviation from requirements but can also be used to tackle an improvement opportunity.

Problems, no matter what their size or complexity, can best be solved by working through a sequence of steps. This ensures that everything possible will be done to apply the available resources in the most effective and efficient manner, consider a number of options and select the best solution.

There are other reasons why such a process is invaluable in group problem-solving:

▦ For people unused to working on improvement teams it is vital to know what the team is currently doing (and not doing). This helps those present to focus on each step in turn rather than seeing their efforts lost with unstructured work.

▦ If the teams are of mixed organisational level and departments a process helps involve those who perhaps because of shyness or lack of seniority would have allowed the noisier elements to dominate the discussion, perhaps to the detriment of the overall team.

There is a structured approach to problem-solving that will help to prevent adverse consequences. Here we shall use the problem-solving process shown in Figure 15.1 which has five clear steps. Many other similar processes are described in the literature (eg Kane (1989)).

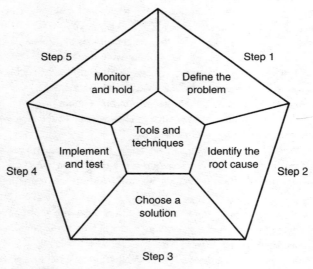

Figure 15.1 *The problem-solving process.*

The advantage to be gained by using such an approach cannot be overstated. Knowing what is expected, what tools to use and generally having a road map for problem-solving helps to prevent problems arising from ill thought-out solutions.

The pentagon highlights the major steps to be taken and poses key questions to be addressed when tackling a problem. The process can be regarded as a continuous cycle.

Once the team has monitored the solution to ensure that the problem is properly solved the members will be able to decide to continue the cycle from Step 1 and seek further improvement or whether the current team should disband and other areas for improvement be addressed.

Since we are describing a process each step has inputs, activities and outputs. The steps and outputs can be viewed as follows.

Step 1: Define the Problem

Problem definition is the most difficult part of problem-solving. There are two main difficulties experienced.

The first is the desire to pick too large a problem to begin with, leading to difficulty expressing and defining the problem. This in turn may mean that different team members have different understandings of the actual problem under consideration.

The second is the propensity to state desired solutions as though they were problems and then the outcome is obvious. An example of this is 'the problem is that we don't have a fax in the office' and the solution 'buy a fax'. These are not problems but 'if we ....' situations.

If we are to solve problems we must have a clear understanding of them and be able to set priorities in order to decide where to start. Many difficulties with problem-solving are caused by people rushing in without understanding what is happening at the time. We can gain that understanding through disciplined analysis.

Problem-solving is simply another form of gap analysis – identifying where we are, identifying where we want to be and then bridging the gap. The 'where we are' can be clearly stated in terms of:

■ a simple definition of the problem – for example: 'complaints due to excessive processing times have risen. We do not know why';
■ quantification of the problem: 'the current level of complaints is running at an average of 50 per week';
■ the who, when, where, how long and any other details available – for example: 'the problem in its present form began in February';
■ the costs caused by the problem – for example: 'additional processing now costs £2,000 per month'.

Once we have defined the problem it can be compared with requirements – what the situation should be:

■ a simple definition of the desired situation, for example a return to the previous situation;
■ quantification of the requirements; for example a target of less than five per week;
■ requirements in terms of who, when, where and how long;
■ the costs when requirements are met, for example the previous level of cost.

The problem is clearly defined as the deviation from requirements, the gap between the current situation and the desired state. Such an assessment leads to direct action towards areas where improvement is most necessary. It also provides a mechanism for measuring success.

Outputs are:

■ a written unambiguous and simple definition;
■ the benefits of solving the problem;

■ a measure of the problem and the desired solution in terms of the gap between the current state and the desired requirements.

Step 2: Find the Root Cause

Many people solve problems by suggesting solutions, testing them and when they fail suggesting another solution. This stems partly from the way people are educated to test hypotheses rather than solve problems and partly from the fact that people believe that they have a 'gut feel' about what is wrong.

This approach is time-consuming and costly and often results in a culture of firefighting. The alternative, of seeking out the root cause of the problem by progressively identifying possible causes and then by analysis and data collection narrowing these down to the actual root cause, may seem long-winded and time-consuming but in the long run is the only guarantee of success.

Long term, the application of techniques in this way can lead from a culture of firefighting to one of fire prevention.

Outputs are:

■ the possible root causes of the problem;
■ data identifying the actual root cause;
■ the root cause of the problem.

Step 3: Choose a Solution

In practice it is not necessarily the best solution to a problem but the solution best applied to a problem that yields optimum results. A solution chosen by a team approach has the commitment of that team behind it and will succeed where 'better' solutions would fail.

Also, solutions to a problem may create problems elsewhere and leave the situation worse than before. One hotel used up old maps after road changes by writing notes on the back of them, only to revert to those maps when the supply of new maps ran out. The problem had only been partially solved and the resulting chaos stemmed from the unwillingness to think through what had to be done to make a solution work.

Outputs are:

■ a list of potential solutions;
■ an analysis of those solutions to determine adverse side-effects;
■ a clear statement of the preferred solution.

Step 4: Implement and Test

It is no good simply having a solution to a problem – the solution needs implementing. This is done by drawing up a plan to implement the solution agreed by the whole team. A word of warning – there are those who at this stage seek to impose the solution that they wanted in the first place. The process can be used to ensure that this is not done.

Like any good plan, this should state who has to do what by when to ensure that all the necessary activities take place.

Once the plan has been implemented we then go on to collect data on the new situation to test that the solution has worked. The benefits of the solution can be measured and communicated to all to demonstrate the achievement.

If the solution has been effective we can go on to the last phase. If not then we need to revisit Step 2 to make certain that the correct root cause was found.

Outputs are:

▪ an agreed implementation plan;
▪ a measure of the benefits gained.

Step 5: Monitor and Hold

Without the status of a permanent change things have a habit of reverting to the previous state when attention is directed elsewhere. To ensure that this does not happen we:

▪ make changes permanent by changing procedures etc;
▪ follow up every change to stop pressures to revert;

here actually happen – do not assume that

y the results;
o everyone.

tc;

ed.

en carrying out any process improvement or
f each step the output does not meet the
vithin the step. It may even be necessary to

s and reasons for decisions and important
eason it is very helpful to keep a log or pro-
n gathered during the work and should 'tell

arise progress to date and to ensure that all
f the problem-solving process that they are

e Problem-solving Process

een explained above, but to generate solu-
there must be some methodology – how do

The answer is in a collection of tools and techniques which encourage creativity in the generation of ideas and useful ways of handling data and making decisions.

A full compendium of tools and techniques will not be given here, but can be found in Kanji and Asher (1996). Figure 15.2 gives examples of the more useful tools and techniques and shows how they fit into the problem-solving process. The matrix indicates at which step of the process the tools are most useful.

	Problem–solving process				
	Step 1	Step 2	Step 3	Step 4	Step 5
Brainstorming	✓	✓	✓	✓	✓
Cause and effect		✓			
Solution effect			✓		
Process flowcharting	✓			✓	
Pareto analysis	✓		✓		
Histograms	✓	✓			
Concentration diagrams	✓	✓			
Checksheets	✓	✓			
Control charts					✓
Scatter diagrams			✓		

Figure 15.2 *Tools and techniques in the problem-solving process.*

ESTABLISHING THE COST OF QUALITY OF THE PROCESS

Once the process flowchart has been established it can then be used to identify the improvement priorities. There are many bases for doing this but one obvious way to proceed is to establish the cost of quality related to the process.

When describing the process it is natural to describe what should happen but there will often be a parallel process that describes what actually happens, the things that go wrong, how they are found to be wrong and how they are corrected.

The costs associated with this 'parallel process' are called the *costs of quality* (Dale and Plunkett, 1991). They are made up of two different types of cost: the *people* costs of quality, relating to people's time spent on the various activities such as chasing and correcting work; and the *accounts* costs of quality, which describe other costs such as audit fees and the cost of maintenance contracts and insurance premiums that are part of the process.

Cost of quality falls naturally into three categories as discussed below.

Prevention Costs

Prevention costs are those costs incurred during the process to ensure that when things happen they happen correctly first time. In other words, prevention activities are those tasks undertaken to prevent the occurrence of failure.

Prevention activities relate to planning, setting goals and objectives, training, writing procedures and all other activities aimed at preventing failure happening.

For example, at home prevention would be setting the fire alarm, buying insurance, painting the woodwork, locking the door. These are all activities undertaken because the consequences of failure – a house fire, replacement costs following a burglary, replacing rotten woodwork or a child running onto a road – are so awful that you are willing to invest in the prevention activities to stop them happening.

On an invoicing process the people costs of quality in the prevention category could be people's time being trained, people's time writing procedures and people's time setting objectives. The accounts costs of quality could be preventative maintenance contracts on equipment or training course fees.

Prevention costs can be looked at as quality investments, carried out as a way of reducing both appraisal and failure costs, thereby reducing the total cost of quality.

Appraisal Costs

Appraisal costs are the costs that are incurred checking whether something is right or wrong, whether work has or has not been performed to the required standard. In other words, prevention costs are before the event, appraisal costs are after the event.

These costs include monitoring performance, checking work, proofreading reports and checking quotations.

The people costs would include time spent sampling invoices, time spent on data collection and time spent analysing information and reporting on progress. The accounts costs would relate to any external expenditures such as those on audit fees or equipment charges.

Failure Costs

Failure costs are those incurred associated with failure to perform work right first time. This will include the disposal or correction of incorrect work and dealing with complaints from customers.

These are therefore the costs that are incurred, for example, when something has gone wrong with the invoicing process, whether internally or externally, and the costs are associated with putting it right. Perhaps the prevention or the appraisal did not work, now the failure has happened, and the process has not been right first time.

Typical failure costs are those to do with chasing for information, being chased for information, dealing with equipment failure, handling irate customers, having to redo work or having to do extra work.

With the invoicing process the people's costs could be time spent correcting invoices, time spent being chased by customers or time spent chasing others for correct information. The accounts costs would include the additional stationery, telephone charges, lost interest on late payments, rush charges and possibly bad debts.

It is possible to split failure costs into internal failure – those costs incurred wholly within the organisation – and external failure – those costs incurred whilst dealing with problems outside the organisation. The author believes that this is unnecessary and can lead to problems simply being moved around rather than solved.

Figure 15.3 provides an example from a client's finance department showing these costs in tabular format.

| | | COST OF QUALITY ESTIMATE | | | | CREDIT CONTROLLER | | | |
| | | APPORTION OF TIME | | | | COST OF QUALITY | | | |
Description of Work Performed	% Time Spent	Normal Work	Prevention	Appraisal	Failure	Normal Work	Prev	App	Fail
(i) Receipt and banking of cheques	5.0	100.0				5.0			
(ii) Posting cash receipts to sales ledger	15.0	100.0				15.0			
(iii) Process credit notes from RCR's received for returned goods, price adjustments, new delay etc.	15.0				100.0				15.0
(iv) Chase payment of overdue DR's using phone/letter/fax etc.	20.0				100.0				20.0
(v) Check statements at the end of each month and highlight overdue sums, export, recent payments etc.	5.0			100.0				5.0	
(vi) Review picking notes rec A/Cs on hold and inform supplier of this situation	5.0			100.0				5.0	
(vii) Deal with customer enquiries re copy invoices. Now deliver and supply the required info.	35.0				100.0				35.0
						20.0	-	10.0	70.0

Figure 15.3 *Cost of quality in a finance department.*

Normal Costs of Business

As well as the costs of quality described above there will be the normal costs associated with invoicing, ie the normal business costs of carrying out the invoicing right first time. These can be illustrated together with the costs of quality as in Figure 15.4.

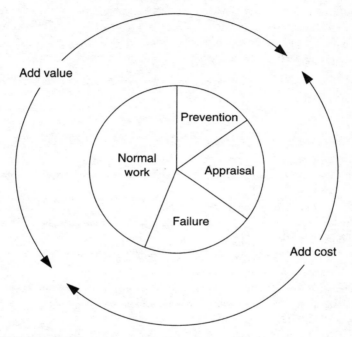

Figure 15.4 *Cost of quality.*

Prevention and the normal costs of business essentially add value to what is done; appraisal and failure only add cost – after all, would you carry out appraisal if you were absolutely certain that everything was right?

Improvement in the process comes from segregating the cost-adding activities from the value-adding activities and then seeking to drive out the activities that only add cost.

In Figure 15.3 it can be seen that 35 per cent of time in the department was spent dealing with copy invoices. This would naturally become an improvement project where the problem-solving process described in the previous section would be used to identify the root causes of the copy invoices and then seek solutions to remove the problem permanently.

In other words, cost of quality can allow people to set priorities for improvement in terms of cost or impact on customer satisfaction. It can also allow people to see their jobs in quality terms and give them the facts to base decisions upon.

The usual reasons for establishing the cost of quality are:

▪ to give a global figure to draw high-level attention to the problem – shock tactics;
▪ to show the high cost areas so allowing the high cost processes to be identified and addressed;
▪ to identify the low cost areas where people might have assumed money was being spent, perhaps allowing future investment in prevention so driving down the total cost;
▪ to demonstrate that quality is a company-wide issue;
▪ to show people that all have a role to play in improvement.

Cost of quality provides an excellent mechanism for surfacing problems which may than be put through the problem-solving process.

UNDERSTANDING INTERNAL CUSTOMERS' NEEDS

One of the major techniques for improving service quality is *department purpose review* (*DPR*).

DPR is important for two main reasons. Firstly, it encourages people in service areas to think about other people within the same organisation as their customers – in many service departments this is not currently the case – and secondly, it provides a structure that can lead to improvement opportunities being identified and then put forward to the steering group for inclusion on the improvement plan.

Additionally, DPR encourages measurement of service activities and leads naturally into team-based improvement activities by way of the problem-solving process described earlier in this chapter.

The DPR process helps members of a department analyse the real purpose of their department and how what they do adds value for the organisation. In particular it builds understanding of:

▪ what the department does and how this fits in with the business needs of the organisation as a whole;
▪ what the departmental priorities are;
▪ what the internal customers of the department actually want and how they perceive what they currently get;
▪ cost of failure within the department and consequent opportunities for improvement;
▪ what needs to be done to bring this about;
▪ how prevention can be planned into what they do to ensure that customer requirements are met in the future.

To do this successfully the team will need a clear understanding of the organisation's mission and vision and how their own goals and roles fit into these.

DPR is a simple six-stage process that takes a departmental team through the following steps:

Step 1: Start-up

The team lists all the activities carried out by the department and agrees the priority order of the activities. At this level we are focusing on the things a department produces, not the tasks carried out to achieve this.

Even at this stage it can reveal differences in understanding within the department of the role and priorities of the department, and resolution of these differences can lead to improvement.

For example, part of the understanding of priorities relates to what to stop doing first when people are absent to ensure that the departmental goals can be met. Having different people taking the decisions with different views of priorities can be very disruptive for the department as a whole. DPR surfaces this problem and allows it to be resolved.

Step 2: Understanding Purpose and Roles

The team then checks with their line manager that there is agreement about both the purpose and priorities of the department.

This can reveal that in fact the manager does not have a clear understanding of what the department does and therefore force this to be discussed.

It could also be found that if the manager has several departments there could be overlap with two departments responsible for the same thing or that whilst the manager had thought that one or other of them was carrying out an activity in fact neither was. For example, when at a meeting figures are called for either two people have produced them and they are different, or no one has produced them.

Step 3: Customer Review

At this stage the customers for each activity are identified and a plan drawn up to go and talk to each of them about their requirements and how well they are being met.

It is wise to develop a list of customers to talk to based on some priority order either of customer or activity, otherwise you can spend all your time doing this at the expense of other work.

At this stage problems will be identified, as will areas where the output you produce is no longer wanted, or where simple changes could have large benefits for your internal customers. Often simple problems are raised which no one thought were problems but knowledge of them assists the improvement of the service provided.

Internal customers often don't complain to you – they just tell everyone else how bad you are! This process brings things into the open for resolution.

Step 4: Time and Cost of Quality Analysis

At this stage you now know what you think you do, what your boss wants you to do and what your customers actually want. We now look at what actually happens in the department. This is done by sampling the tasks people carry out and then (using the categories described earlier in the chapter) categorise them as prevention, appraisal, failure and normal work.

The failure and appraisal activities add no value to what the department does, they only add cost.

Step 5: Action Plan

Having established the cost-adding activities this stage involves planning to reduce them, perhaps by investing in prevention.

There are generally two types of activity at this stage – those relating to work that is done that does not fit in with what the department is for and what its customers want, and those relating to activities that are needed but are done inefficiently or ineffectively.

This stage of the process may mean going back to Step 3 (customers) or Step 2 (the manager) to renegotiate requirements.

Step 6: Prevention

Having driven failure out of the system the team then takes a fresh look at their activities in terms of what can be done to build prevention into their activities rather than relying on checking to reveal errors.

This focus on prevention helps the move towards continuous improvement.

Benefits and Drawbacks of DPR

DPR can bring many benefits to an organisation. The main ones are:

■ a better understanding of departmental roles;
■ an emphasis on measurement;
■ a training aid for new members of the department;
■ an aid for a new departmental manager;
■ an emphasis on the idea of internal customers;
■ a focus for improvement projects.

There is a possible danger of becoming too introspective and thereby spending too much time identifying and working on internal customer relationships at the expense of the external customer. Provided that this is recognised and the role of the internal customer in serving the external customer is emphasised, there should be no real problems.

The technique helps service departments see themselves as just that and the emphasis on customers is an excellent focus for improvement.

DPR also provides a mechanism for surfacing problems for later resolution.

16

OPPORTUNITIES FOR INNOVATION

Opportunities for innovation stem from many sources. These include:;

- the unexpected successes or failures that we have, and unexpected outside events, for example the end of the Cold War;
- incongruity, for example incongruous economic realities, differences between actual and perceived customer or staff values and expectations;
- a sudden need to improve the process because of failure;
- a change in the outside market that forces change, for example British Telecom following Mercury's entry;
- changes to the population and the needs of the population, for example changes to the number of single-person families make it difficult to enter to read meters;
- changes in perception – people no longer expect new cars to go wrong;
- new knowledge or technology – the cable network is an example of this.

It is often difficult to change the way that things are done simply because that is the way that they have always been done. The inertia of the system militates against change. This often comes through in phrases like 'We've always done it that way' and 'How else could it be done?'

Every now and then someone comes along and fundamentally challenges the status quo, resulting in a change in the way people view things from then on. Changes of this nature – such as the mobile phone which means that you phone a person not a place, Direct Line which has changed completely the nature of selling insurance, Virgin which challenged assumptions about crossing the Atlantic – may need a catalyst to bring them about.

The three examples above are not tinkering about at the edges, they are *fundamentally shifting* the way people think. Afterwards the world will not be the same.

Thinking the unthinkable can be difficult and it is helpful to have some techniques to help with this. There is a wide range of such techniques available for encouraging creative thinking to bring about innovative solutions to the problems facing business today, whether in the public or private sector. The following example – Imagineering – has been used with considerable success across a varied range of business environments.

IMAGINEERING

Imagineering assists in identifying areas of opportunity by concentrating on the ideal outcome and then working back from it. It therefore provides support when clarifying the vision and builds a list of actions required when planning what has to be done to achieve the vision.

Imagineering is a simple five-step process as follows:

1. Brainstorm a list of characteristics that indicate the ideal situation. This list can be developed in a group with all of those familiar with or experienced in the process involved.
2. For each of the characteristics identified, state the actual current situation.
3. For each of the characteristics identified, identify the gap to be bridged to bring about the ideal situation.
4. Use 'cause and effect analysis' to break down the gap into small areas that can be identified. These areas can be categorised in various ways. One popular set of major headings is 'People', 'Equipment', 'Methods' and 'Materials'.
5. For each of the small areas identified, agree an owner and timescale for completion.

Benefits

The benefits of imagineering are that it takes the ideal situation and breaks it down into a list of actions which, if achieved, will bring about the desired change. The strength is that it breaks down what can be seen as a daunting task into a list of actions that can be achieved by individuals or small teams. An example will illustrate how this works in practice.

Suppose the manager of a high street bank working on a customer care programme is working out the ideal situation for the bank's customers. The first stage is to brainstorm and list ideal characteristics:

Ideal:
- customers receive a warm greeting;
- attentive service;
- pleasant environment;
- privacy when required; etc.

The next stage is to identify the actual current situation in each of these desired characteristics:

Actual:
- the staff are unfriendly;
- the service is slow;
- the surroundings are dingy;
- there is an open plan layout; etc.

The third stage for each of the characteristics is to identify the gaps and their causes. Figure 16.1 shows how this may be depicted.

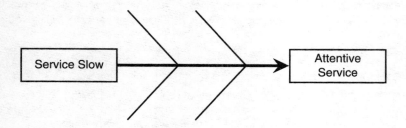

Figure 16.1 *The imagineering diagram.*

For each of the constituent parts a plan is then drawn up and ownership and timescales agreed to bridge the gap.

STARTING WITH A CLEAN SHEET

The industrial model of business is predicated on the belief that workers have few skills and that tasks must be broken down into small, discrete, blocks. This allows tasks to be simple and repetitive and has its origins in Adam Smith's belief that people work most effectively when they have one easily understood task to perform.

Simple tasks unfortunately demand complex processes to bring them together. This has led to organisations accepting the inconvenience, inefficiency and excessive cost associated with complex processes – because they want to benefit from simple tasks.

The contemporary world demands flexibility, service, superior quality and low cost. To deliver this, processes must be kept simple and responsive. This has enormous implications for how processes are designed and organisations are shaped.

These are commonly recurring themes that become apparent in re-engineered business processes.

Jobs Are Combined

There are two ways of assessing the time to carry out a process – the process work time and the process elapsed time.

Imagine a circumstance where an enquiry comes into an organisation and is logged by one individual. The process work time is two minutes.

The enquiry is then passed on to the stores where a check is made about whether the item is in or out of stock. The process work time is three minutes.

The enquiry is passed onto the stores picker who gets the item from the stores. The process work time is five minutes.

Then into packing – only a five-minute job – into despatch and the item is sent to the customer.

The process work time is:

Logging   –   2 minutes

Checking –   3 minutes

Picking   –   5 minutes

Packing   –   5 minutes

Total   –   15 minutes

However, the elapsed process time could be several days, as the enquiry is passed from one individual in one department to another in another department. If the elapsed time was three days, the process work time would less than 1 per cent of the total elapsed time. Imagine paperwork processes or data processes where there are many more steps – the end result would be worse still.

There are other disadvantages too. Because the process involves so many steps, errors and misunderstandings are inevitable. No one can see the total process, so when customers present enquiries no one can help them.

The new process would combine all of the jobs in the process into one. The person holding that job could 'walk through' the order from enquiry to fulfilment, and would also be the contact point for the customer should the need arise. Since things typically go wrong between individuals or departments the benefits are clear. No longer do things 'fall between two stools' – the job is done on one stool.

There are other benefits too. A substantial part of the administrative work was involved in recording the process itself – to prove that the document had moved. This would no longer be necessary with only one person dealing with all of the steps.

Simpler processes mean fewer process faults and therefore fewer people involved with fixing problems. In this way the work is of better quality.

For larger or more complex processes the approach might be to have a 'case team' where the team rather than one individual is responsible for carrying out the process. In this case the team members would have all of the necessary skills to execute the total process. Studies suggest that using a 'case worker' or 'case team' makes a process operate *ten times* faster.

An extension of this approach would be to have a case manager as the single point of contact for outside enquiries. To handle this task efficiently, full access to all information is vital and the role of information technology becomes important. An organisation under severe pressure to reduce its shipment times found that this approach reduced the time to despatch assembled products from three days to three hours.

Decisions Delegated to Those Doing the Work

Case workers or case teams compress processes horizontally by performing many sequential tasks, so transforming simple tasks held together by complex processes into complex tasks held together by simple processes.

One facet of the Adam Smith organisation was that those doing the work, process workers, were separated from those taking decisions about the work, managers. Instead of separating decision-taking from work, processes may be changed to make taking the decisions part of that work. In place of passing decisions upwards for resolution, decisions are taken 'on the job' by the case workers or case team.

The old assumption was that workers lacked the knowledge and skills to take decisions and lacked the inclination to do so. The new organisation delegates decision-making and gives people the skills to take decisions on their process.

There are many beneficial side-effects of this. Firstly, the hierarchy that was built up to make decisions – supervisors, auditors, managers – can be slimmed down because they have fewer decisions to take. Secondly, since decisions are taken when they need to be taken, the process will necessarily be faster because there will be no waiting for others to take decisions. There is also a morale benefit from the giving of more complete jobs to people and showing the full picture rather than only one part.

The reduced number of organisational levels and fewer delays means lower costs stemming from lower overheads and improved customer satisfaction. So, as well as horizontal compression of processes there is also vertical compression.

Changes in the Order of Process Steps to Reflect the Work Being Done

The consequence of one task having to be performed before another, of one department carrying out the work before another, inevitably leads to delays.

An example of this involves an organisation, part of a major industrial conglomerate, supplying automotive components. The organisation viewed new product introduction as a sequential process whereby the steps were carried out in a well-defined order. The steps in the first stage of the process 'Generating a Sales Requirement' were:

1. Generate a sales requirement.
2. Compile a technical data sheet.
3. Validate the project.
4. Raise a cost request.
5. Authorise the cost request.
6. Estimation of market size.
7. Project authorisation.
8. Compile cost questionnaire.
9. Complete cost questionnaire.
10. Study and analyse costing.

11. Compile bill of materials.
12. Produce quotation request.
13. Produce tooling estimate request.
14. Calculate materials and labour cost.
15. Complete standard costing.
16. Complete feasibility study.
17. Release information to Sales.

Sitting alongside this were other processes around production – drawings, production schedules, manufacture, despatch and invoicing. Each department did its own work and then passed it on to the next. The effect was that a target of 14 days for the total process gave an actual performance of between 28 and 70 days. Each department only saw the one part.

The organisation realised that the steps did not have to be sequential but could run in parallel. Firstly, parts of the sales process itself could run in parallel. Secondly, the other departmental processes could begin at the same time and run in parallel with the sales process.

The benefits were enormous. The amount of time taken reduced dramatically to ten days and the organisation was better able to cope with any necessary changes, thereby reducing the costs of work having to be repeated and the time involved.

The major realisation was that some steps could begin without having to wait for others to be completed.

Multiple Versions of Processes Allowed

Processes, recipes and procedures have the joint aims of consistency and repeatability. The intention is that error is driven out of a process by having 'one best way'. This was the idea behind mass production – all inputs were handled identically so that uniform and consistent work would be produced.

With mass market customisation, the move is towards doing one thousand things once, not one thing a thousand times. This is done by having multiple versions of the same process, each tuned to meet different demands.

The previous example of the automotive components supplier illustrates this point well. Whether the demand was for a new alternator to sell five million units per year in the replacement market, for a new fixing bracket or for an original part to sell only 20,000 a year, the process was the same.

The organisation developed three separate processes to deal with the three types of request, thereby making sure that work was not wasted producing information that would not be used. The first step of the process was to decide which process to use. The improvements were substantial. Since the major process was not being 'clogged up' by more trivial requests it became much faster and more efficient. Secondly, minor requests could be dealt with in less than five days since they no longer had to go through the total process.

Customer satisfaction improved as customers were dealt with more on the merits of the individual requests than being forced to take their place in the queue.

Work Performed in the Right Place

A manager's first task is to build a department, a hierarchy of specialists to deal with specialist requests. Pay will depend on department size rather then organisational efficiency so it was wise to draw tasks within the department.

In consequence, people use specialists to do what they could do for themselves. One large insurance company discovered it was running a travel agency because the long-term effect of requests for airline bookings was a department to do that very necessary task.

The organisation put back the booking of flights to the departments using the service, thus saving on the cost of the internal travel agency. Previously, including overheads, it had cost £80 per reservation made. It was more efficient to use a local, approved, travel agency and cost far less. In addition, travellers spent less time making the bookings and then changing them.

It may be possible, via market testing or competitive tendering, to delegate the process entirely and use an external supplier to do the work more efficiently and less expensively.

One large cigarette manufacturer asks their supplier of cartons to estimate the next month's requirements using historical data and to tell them what they are producing. The two organisations share data and the cigarette company believes that the carton maker will do the job as well as they could. This has the effects of blurring the boundaries between an organisation and its suppliers.

It can also operate the other way with customers. Toyota builds cars – they also build houses. They have developed a design process that gets the customer to design their own house and the design document is input directly into the manufacturing process. This makes the process faster, easier and gives the customer exactly what is wanted.

Checking and Monitoring Reduced

One role of organisational hierarchy is to provide checks and balances to ensure that people are not abusing the process. In many organisations signatures on signatures are commonplace where in practice one person signs because another already has done so.

The case of a steel producer illustrates this, where a manager must sign a travel request which then goes to a senior manager who must sign and, depending upon the amount, this can go up to chief executive level. In total a request could collect 12 signatures.

Whilst done for good reasons, and particularly so in the public sector when public money is at stake, the costs of the process are large and the delays introduced can be long. A circumstance where the cost of checking could exceed the value of the goods or services bought can easily be envisaged. This can lead to a blind eye being used and people bending the system and documentation being put in place later.

The modern process has checks and controls but these tend to be of a different nature. An example is the international airline business where travellers can switch from one carrier to another and money goes with them. In the past, carriers used to set up complex methods of accounting for all transfers with all other carriers and then bill amounts and collect. Naturally, this was also happening the other way.

All carriers took a decision that travellers on routes were as likely to switch one way as another so, on average, the balance would be equal. The decision was made to stop all cross billing and monitor the situation on a sample basis that the balance was being maintained. Therefore all the costs of cross billing and collection were avoided as the activity ceased.

There is always a decision to be taken. There may be abuse, but are the costs associated with finding it greater than the money saved? Modern processes tolerate moderate and limited abuse as a way of reducing costs.

Reconciliation Reduced

The manager writes out the order and sends it to purchasing. Purchasing log the order, issue an order number, arrange a supplier and send the order to the area where the goods will arrive. On arrival the order number will be checked against the goods and description and the completed document will be sent to purchasing, the manager who originated the order and accounts.

The supplier now has three points of contact – the manager, accounts and purchasing – and three possibilities for error. Each document has to reconcile with others. Having one external contact would reduce this and make the process more certain.

Decentralised Operations

Try telephoning a large multinational company and asking for information. They will probably tell you that you are speaking to the wrong part of the organisation and give you another contact. Unfortunately, you will probably get the same response. Eventually you will get tired of this and go elsewhere.

There is no reason, with the technology available, why the sales process of the organisation should pay any attention to boundaries that the customers do not see. The same activities using the same processes could exist across the organisational boundaries, sharing technology to best effect.

REALIGNING THE PROCESS TO CUSTOMER NEEDS

Processes exist to satisfy customer needs. However good the service and its delivery, if the customer perception of the quality is at variance with the actual quality then, inevitably, the perception remains.

There are two elements of quality – customer perceived quality and the needs of the market. This approach is market orientated, and externally orientated with the focus on the customer. The centre of the model is the customer's perception of quality. This is affected by the customer's expectations, which are related to past experiences.

Perceived quality is also affected by image and reputation. An image can be better or worse than the real thing, but it acts as a filter for perceived quality.

Perceived quality as a concept is difficult to grasp because it contains both objective and subjective factors and is dependent on the characteristic features of the customer – education, values, state of mind. To improve quality we must therefore influence expectations, experience and image. Quality improvement is not always directly about the service or product offered.

For customers to have a satisfactory perception of the service offered the *design quality* must be correct. This relates to how a product or service has been developed and put together.

It is not only the quality of the offering that must be defined, it is just as important to define the level of quality. The customers must be involved in the definition, be they patients, clients, consumers or users.

It must be apparent to all that, for example, an outpatients' department at a typical hospital has not been designed for the benefit of patients, but for the benefit of consultants. Consider the facts: patients park furthest away, consultants nearest. There are levels of filters – receptionists being the first – to keep patients away. The general process dehumanises patients.

It does not have to be this way, but for a real change to happen the hospital would have to change completely its vision of what the organisation is there for.

To start at the beginning: a hospital is a building. Patients go there for a variety of reasons, of which outpatients is one. Why must a patient go to outpatients in the first place? Is a visit to a hospital necessary to change a dressing?

The whole process could be changed to centre around patient needs, resulting in improved patient satisfaction, lower cost and improved use of an expensive resource. The change would thus be from a specialist-centred process to a patient-centred process, starting from customer needs which are then driven back in the organisation through a series of internal customer/supplier links to develop a process to meet those needs.

We should start with what the customer wants, not with what the organisation can offer. We can find out what is wanted in a variety of ways, by questionnaires, discussions, market research, external comparisons and sampling, all aimed at developing a specification to describe customer needs.

As well as customers, staff and other stakeholders – for example, government, local or national – also have an input to the design. It is not easy to achieve quality with so many groups involved, but their needs need not be incongruent and they often coincide.

IN SUMMARY

Whatever happens, competition continues. In a dynamic marketplace on the world stage, organisations that learn, learn that nothing fails like success.

As the market changes so does the mission, the critical success factors and the key processes. Successful organisations recognise this and keep on changing.

17

CASE STUDY: TRUMPLINGTON HEALTH AUTHORITY

BACKGROUND

Trumplington Health Authority was established as a new health authority in April 1994 as part of the government's NHS reforms. The new role of the health authority is to purchase health care for the resident population of Dumplington based on an assessment of the health needs of the population.

In October 1994 the government made a further announcement as part of the NHS reforms. With effect from April 1996 health authorities would be merged with their sister health authorities, the Family Health Services Authorities. Family Health Services Authorities have responsibility for the local implementation of nationally negotiated contracts for the providers of family health services, namely general practitioner services, general dental services, pharmaceutical services (chemists), and optical services (opticians).

In anticipation of the new proposals, agreement was reached between Trumplington Health Authority and the two family health services authorities which relate to the health authority to bring together all the activities of the three health organisations into one integrated organisation.

The new health organisation covers a resident population of 446,300 and spends £252 m on health care for that population. The Health Authority buys health services from eight main providers (trusts) and 242 general practitioners, 192 general dentists, 113 chemists and 112 opticians.

The purchasing of health care can also be carried out by general practitioner fundholders who purchase a more limited range of services for their population but it is important that the health authorities work closely with the fundholders to ensure that health targets are achieved across the whole population and that services do not become fragmented. By April 1996 47 per cent of the population of Dumplington will have their health care purchased by fundholders. Money allocated to fundholders comes off the Health Authority allocation, leaving the Health Authority to purchase health care for the rest of the population with the remaining monies.

The three health authorities are very committed to working together in anticipation of

172 ■ Managing Quality in the Service Sector

the April 1996 changes and have agreed a joint mission and identified joint values and aims:

MISSION

- To improve the health of Trumplington people.
- To improve the quality of health care received by Trumplington people.
- To get the best value for the money spent on the health of Trumplington people.

VALUES

- Health is not only the absence of disease; it is physical, mental and emotional well-being.
- Resources to improve health are not just in the health sector. They are in individuals, families, communities and other organisations.
- Improving health depends on involving local people and organisations outside the NHS.
- Effective health care should be care given to people in the community, supported by hospital care only where necessary.
- Care for people with long-term needs should promote their independence and should support them in their own homes if possible.

AIMS

The key purpose of health improvement is to:

- reduce inequalities by improving the health of the most disadvantaged people;
- improve the overall health of the population; and
- increase the power and choice of individuals and communities.

The key purpose of improving services for Trumplington people is to ensure they are:

▪ accessible in ways and places that make it easy for people to use them;
▪ acceptable to Trumplington people;
▪ relevant to the needs of Trumplington people;
▪ fair in meeting the different needs of different groups;
▪ effective in improving health; and
▪ efficient in the way they use money and other resources.

ORGANISATION

The management arrangements in respect of the organisation are as follows.

▪ Chief Executive
▪ Executive Directors × 5
  − Finance/Information/Registration
  − Public Health/Health of the Nation
  − Contracting/Patient's Charter
  − Organisational Development/GP Fundholding
  − Primary and Community Care/Administration
▪ Associate Directors × 10
▪ Senior Managers × 24
▪ Administrative Staff × 38
▪ Clerical Staff × 44

These are shown in the organisation chart in Figure 17.1.

CRITICAL SUCCESS FACTORS

The management executive recognise that if they are to achieve their mission they would need to identify the critical factors which should be in place. During a half-day brain-storming exercise the team came up with the following list of potential critical success factors.

▪ accurate information about the health status of the people of Trumplington;
▪ a way of analysing this information;
▪ an agreement on the priorities for action;
▪ accurate information about the health services which are currently provided for the people of Trumplington;
▪ what standards are currently in place in respect of the providers of health care including hospital services, community services, GP services, etc.;
▪ the location of the service providers in relation to the population;
▪ how much money is spent on health care;

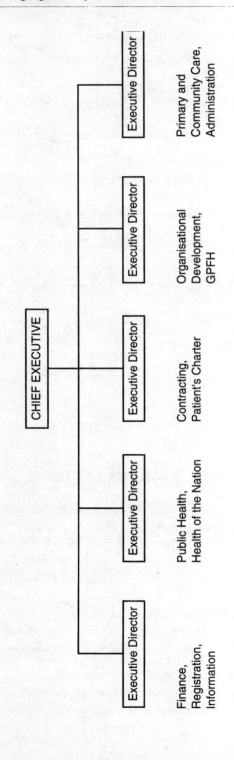

Figure 17.1 *Trumplington Health Authority – organisation chart.*

▪ ways of linking in with the people of Trumplington;
▪ ways of working with the GP fundholders;
▪ ways of working with the providers of health care;
▪ ways of working with the two local authorities;
▪ ways of identifying alternative providers of health care;
▪ ways of assessing the suitability of alternative providers;
▪ ways of measuring whether what the Health Authority is purchasing is effective.

Of these the management executive agreed that the critical success factors were:

▪ excellent communications with the community;
▪ excellent working relationship with the GP fund holders;
▪ excellent monitoring systems for activity and cash performance of the providers;
▪ a skilled and well-motivated workforce;
▪ effective ways of getting key messages across to stakeholders.

THE BUSINESS PROCESSES

The management executive have identified five key business processes to help them deliver the critical success factors and hence the mission. These will incorporate the agreed values and aims as follows:

▪ focusing on desired change – orientating the players;
▪ developing the market – improving the capability of the players;
▪ managing the market – regulating the behaviour of the players;
▪ monitoring the market – knowing what's going on/checking it's happening;
▪ developing and managing the new organisation – improving our capability/efficiency.

These are core processes for Trumplington. They involve all parts of the organisation. In some cases these processes reach outside the organisation into the local authority and Community Health Council areas of control.

Each of these key business processes is supported by a group of sub-processes which the management executive identified as follows.

Focusing on Desired Change – Orientating the Players

1. *Analysing Annual Purchasing Intentions*. This is an analysis, contract by contract, of the implications for activity and price of proposed purchasing intentions for the following financial year. The analysis includes the effect of proposed changes on efficiency and on provider viability.
2. *Developing Purchasing Plans/GPFH Plans*. The annual purchasing plan includes a review of the previous and current years' proposals/changes, consideration of responses on the purchasing intentions after consultation, discussions with GPFHs

about areas of common interest, analysis of GPFH proposals, consideration of the community care plans and children's services plans produced by the local authorities, a review of work in hand including identification of achievements of objectives set by the Department of Health.

3. *Developing Community Care Plans*. Lead responsibility for producing the community care plan rests with the local authority but it must be compatible with the purchasing plan of the Health Authority and with the GPFH plans.

4. *Developing Children's Services Plans*. Lead responsibility rests with the local authority and must be compatible with the Health Authority purchasing plans and GPFH plans.

5. *Agreeing the Annual Corporate Contract*. Each year the health authorities undergo a review by the regional tier of the Department of Health and each year health authorities are given actions to perform by which they will be assessed.

6. *Developing Health of the Nation/Healthy Alliances*. The local Health Authority has to identify how it will take forward the government's strategy for health by demonstrating links with other agencies.

7. *Consulting on Proposed Service Changes with the Public*. Where the Health Authority proposes to make substantial service changes it is required to conform to a set procedure for consulting with the general public on such changes.

8. *Involving the Public in the Decision-making Process*. If the Health Authority is to truly identify the population's needs it needs to set up mechanisms which allow the Health Authority to explain its proposals and to take on board comments and suggestions put forward by the people.

9. *Identifying and Assessing Health*. Identifying health needs of the population by using information available from the providers of health care, the Office of National Statistics (ONS) and other central information gathering organisations.

10. *Developing Knowledge-based Local Purchasing*. Review of clinical effectiveness, development of local intelligence, identification of areas for disinvestment based on clinical evidence, research reviews, clinical outcome assessment, health technology assessment.

11. *Specifying New Local Contracts*. The development of improved contract specification based on processes 9 and 10.

12. *Setting Annual Resource Allocation and Budgets*. The annual cycle of responding to the allocation of finance to the Health Authority as part of the annual expenditure round including internal budget setting, contract pricing, identification of contingencies, risk analysis, assessment of overall efficiency, and assessment of overall efficiency gain.

Developing the Market – Improving the Capability of the Players

13. *Extending the Coverage and Scope of the GPFHs*. Identifying and developing criteria for practices wishing to join the GPFH scheme and assessing their suitability against the criteria. Developing action plans for practices to enable them to meet all

the criteria during the preparatory year. Interpreting national guidance in respect of fundholding and recommending application to existing/developing fundholding practices. Developing and implementing agreement with fundholding practices on the use of management allowances, the timetable for developing purchasing intentions, business plans, annual reports, the use of savings, monitoring arrangements, and resource allocation policies.

14. *Training/Development of GPFH/GPs/Health Care Teams.* If the Health Authority is to ensure that more care is provided in the community then it will need to develop the capacity of the community-based health care providing teams. Each practice or team will have a development plan with specific targets against which progress can be measured.

15. *Training of External NHS Staff/Students.* The Health Authority derives income from providing training to NHS trainees. The placements should be within a structure which includes an induction programme, placement objectives and assessment processes.

16. *Developing a Framework for Joint Working with the Local Authorities.* There are two separate local authorities with whom the Health Authority needs to work in producing community care plans and children's services plans. The statutory agencies need to agree policies for providing care in the community and identify the roles and responsibilities of the key players.

17. *Developing a Framework for Joint Working with Other Health Authorities.* No single provider of health care derives all its income from just one health purchaser. As a consequence there is great value in health purchasers working together, particularly if there are questions about the long-term viability or sustainability of some providers.

18. *Developing a Framework for Research and Development.* The Health Authority will need to initiate local research, particularly if it is to purchase effective health care. A system for initiating research and then implementing findings is required.

19. *Developing a Framework for Professional Education/Training.* Whilst professional education and training is largely coordinated outside of the health authority's control there is an increasing recognition that health authorities need to have an input into this activity.

20. *Hospital Site Rationalisation.* Working with other health care purchasers to identify and evaluate the options for the pattern of hospital provision.

21. *Agreeing Capital Investments in Hospital and Community Health Services.* Assessing and advising on capital proposals put forward by the providers.

22. *Developing More Sophisticated Contracts for HCHS.* The Health Authority needs to develop a better understanding of the outputs it obtains for its investment and then define requirements via contracts for health care

23. *Improving GP Premises.* In line with developing the capacity of the community providers of health care comes the need to develop a way of improving GP premises where the GP is the owner of the premises and may not wish to invest his/her own money for this.

24. *Controlling Costs of GP Staffing.* There are earmarked sums available for the contribution towards the cost of staff employed by GPs. The use of these resources is

extremely variable, and the Health Authority needs to develop criteria for allocating these monies.

25. *Supporting GP Computing Strategies.* The specification, design, implementation and support of information technology to assist GP practices.

26. *Ensuring Cost-effective Prescribing/New Drugs.* Ensure that all GPs have agreed action plans for using the prescribing allocation and that these are monitored and reviewed. Establish mechanisms which allow shared care between hospitals and GPs. Establish information systems which provide intelligence and information on new drugs which have potentially significant clinical and/or financial implications.

27. *Clinical Audit/Guidelines/Protocols for Shared GP/Consultant Care.* Develop, agree and implement shared care agreements between GPs and hospital consultants which can also be measured to ensure that care is provided on the basis of effectiveness.

Managing the Market – Regulating the Behaviour of the Players

28. *Negotiating HCHS Contracts.* Negotiation with the providers of hospital and community health services to agree price activity and services to be delivered. Also includes ongoing discussions with providers in order to establish relationships.

29. *Implementing Contract Changes to HCHS and Family Health Services.* The process of negotiating service changes arising from whatever source including national imperatives.

30. *Identifying Areas for Market Testing.* Identification of areas for market testing. Write service specification. Proceed to tender, evaluate, review and award contract.

31. *Reducing Waiting Times.* The process of ensuring that waiting time targets required by the centre are met as a minimum requirement for the residents of Dumplington.

32. *Promoting Service Alliances/Package Contracts between Trusts.* The promotion of service alliances between providers of health care. Services to be delivered in the most appropriate setting and by the most appropriate provider.

33. *Controlling Extra Contractual Referrals (ECRs).* To control the entry/exit of providers of services for HCHS using effectiveness/value/appropriateness of that provider. Within the financial budget manage the process of authorising, approving for payment, monitoring and maintenance of the Extra Contractual Referral process. The process should include regular reports to the Director of Finance and should highlight problems in the system.

34. *Arbitrating Local Disputes between GPFH and Providers.* This involves the arbitration of contract disputes between the fundholding practices and individual providers of NHS care.

35. *Agreeing Support Plans/Contracts between the Health Authority and Family Health Service Providers/GPFHs.* To develop joint purchasing between the Health Authority and Family Health Service Providers, including GPFHs.

36. *Developing Entry/Exit Policy On GPFHs/Family Health Service Providers.*

Develop local policies for purchasing family health services. Provide advice on the implications of implementing locally developed contracts.

37. *Locality Market Making.* This involves the development of mechanisms for the process of involving GPs and other primary care providers in the process of purchasing and in discussions as providers. It will need to include the development of a locality-based approach to both health needs assessment and the provision of services.

38. *Inspecting/Registering Nursing Homes.* The Health Authority is responsible for the registration of nursing homes and for their regular inspection. It also entails liaison with the local authority who are responsible for the registration of residential care homes and who now purchase the majority of places in nursing homes.

39. *Paying HCHS Providers.* The payment to Trusts for patient and other services provided in accordance the plans, policies and procedures of the Health Authority.

40. *Paying FHS Providers.* The payment to GPs, dentists, opticians and pharmacists for the services which they provide in accordance with the nationally negotiated contracts.

41. *Registering Patient Data.* The maintenance of a register of patients registered with GPs practising in Dumplington.

Monitoring the Market – Knowing What's Going on/ Checking it's Happening

42. *Developing Annual Public Health Report/Surveillance.* The process of monitoring and reporting on the health status of the people of Dumplington. This includes examining routine published data and commissioning surveys.

43. *Monitoring Communicable Disease Control/HIV/Immunisation.* Surveillance of communicable diseases including HIV/AIDS. Coordination of the immunisation programme.

44. *Monitoring and Controlling Environmental Health.* Surveillance of illness and disease caused/influenced by environmental factors. Provision of professional advice on environmental hazards, chemical incidents and radiation incidents.

45. *Accessing Health Literature.* Making effective use of the in-house library of textual material including electronic access to large databases.

46. *Monitoring HCHS Expenditure.* Monitoring expenditure on hospital and community health services in accordance with the agreed contracts.

47. *Monitoring FHS Expenditure.* Monitoring expenditure on services provided by GPs, dentists, opticians and pharmacists.

48. *Monitoring HSCS Activity.* Monitoring activity levels for hospital and community health services to ensure that efficiency targets are reached.

49. *Monitoring FHS Activity.* Monitoring the activities of GPs, dentists, opticians and pharmacists particularly in relation to health screening and disease prevention programmes.

50. *Monitoring Patient Charter Standards and Other Affordable Standards.* The process of ensuring that services purchased from all providers reach acceptable standards and that Charter Standards are met.

51. *Monitoring Contract Outcomes*. To develop the contracting process in terms of documentation, financial data and activity data to focus on outcomes of health care rather than the process details contained in the current contracts. Contracts should also move to procedure specific or volume/cash sensitive better to meet the health needs of the population.

52. *Complaints/Litigation/Responding to Enquiries*. Ensure that effective systems are in place for the handling of all complaints/litigation/enquiries.

Developing and Managing the New Organisation – Improving our Capability/Efficiency

54. *Developing Human Resource Policies/Health and Safety at Work*. Develop, agree and implement common human resource policies across the Health Authority. Ensure statutory requirements for health and safety at work are met.

55. *Single Management System/Performance Review/Organisational Development*. Develop an effective and efficient management structure which enables the functions of the authorities to be performed. Develop and implement management processes across the Health Authority which enable standards to be established and monitored which improve service delivery.

56. *Training/Team Building/Standard Procedures*. Develop and implement a training strategy which supports the goals and aims of the Health Authority and enables individuals to achieve their optimum capabilities.

57. *Communicating Policies*. Ensure effective systems are in place which facilitate good external and internal communications including the development and implementation of a communications strategy which identifies the ways in which the Health Authority will relate to their own staff and externally.

58. *Administration/Secretariat/Supplies*. Ensure that the Health Authority is properly supported by administrative services including secretarial and administrative support, purchasing of supplies, servicing of meetings and postal services.

59. *Accommodation/Fire Safety*. Determination of matters relating to accommodation including health and safety, security, car parking and telephones.

60. *Corporate Governance/Compliance with Statute/Probity*. Provision of advice on standing financial instructions, probity and corporate governance.

61. *Financial and Management Accounts*. Ensure that the statutory duty to account for income expenditure and fixed assets is discharged to professional standards. To set budgets and contracts in accordance with the policies and financial strategy of the Health Authority.

62. *Auditing Internal/External Systems*. Ensure internal and external audit is conducted to proper professional standards.

63. *Designing and Specifying Information Technology*. Specification, design, implementation and support of information technology to assist the business of the Health Authority.

64. *Coordination of Business/Organisational Library/Management of Chief Executive's*

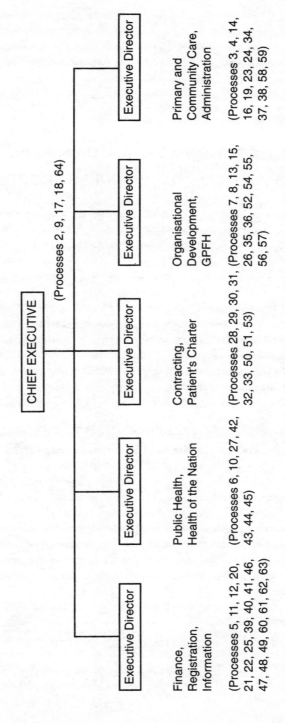

Figure 17.2 *Allocation of processes.*

Office. The CE's office is the main focus for relationships between the Health Authority and external agencies. It is a channel of communication between the outside world and directors with particular management responsibilities. It is therefore a major entry point to the organisation for textual-based information. This process involves the development of integrated text management strategies and a common filing system to promote effective corporate management and the coordination of business.

Processes are allocated to executives as shown in Figure 17.2.

ASSESSMENT OF THE BUSINESS PROCESSES

The management team had a two-day workshop to allow them to consider the critical success factors, the key processes and the quality of operation of those processes.

They first of all scored the processes against the success factors as shown in Figure 17.3.

Following this they scored the major processes and then determined the quality ratings as in Figure 17.4.

It can be seen that whilst the organisation was very good at managing itself there were several areas particularly relating to the external market where processes that had a major contribution to the success factors were being performed extremely badly.

One such sub-process was number 33 – the method by which extra contractual referrals was controlled. Accordingly the Authority set up an improvement team to look for ways of bringing about an improvement.

IMPROVEMENT WORK ON PROCESS 33: CONTROLLING EXTRA CONTRACTUAL REFERRALS (ECRS)

Process Description

Within the financial budget and subject to the overall policy of the Health Authority, to manage the process of authorisation, approval for payment, monitoring and maintenance of the ECR process. The process shall include regular reports to the Executive Director (Finance) and shall highlight problems in the system, especially financial over-commitment.

Background

Whilst the Health Authority purchases most health care for the residents of Dumplington from seven major providers of services, there are situations where requests are made for

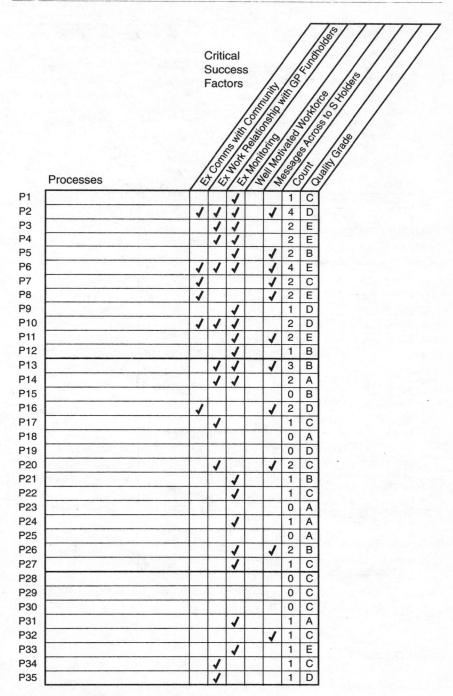

Processes	Ex Comms with Community	Ex Work Relationship with GP Fundholders	Ex Monitoring	Well Motivated Workforce	Messages Across to S Holders	Count	Quality Grade
P1			✓			1	C
P2	✓	✓	✓		✓	4	D
P3		✓	✓			2	E
P4		✓	✓			2	E
P5			✓		✓	2	B
P6	✓	✓	✓		✓	4	E
P7	✓				✓	2	C
P8	✓				✓	2	E
P9			✓			1	D
P10	✓	✓	✓			2	D
P11			✓		✓	2	E
P12			✓			1	B
P13		✓	✓		✓	3	B
P14		✓	✓			2	A
P15						0	B
P16	✓				✓	2	D
P17		✓				1	C
P18						0	A
P19						0	D
P20		✓			✓	2	C
P21				✓		1	B
P22				✓		1	C
P23						0	A
P24				✓		1	A
P25						0	A
P26				✓	✓	2	B
P27				✓		1	C
P28						0	C
P29						0	C
P30						0	C
P31				✓		1	A
P32					✓	1	C
P33				✓		1	E
P34		✓				1	C
P35		✓				1	D

Critical Success Factors

Figure 17.3 *Scoring of processes against critical success factors.*

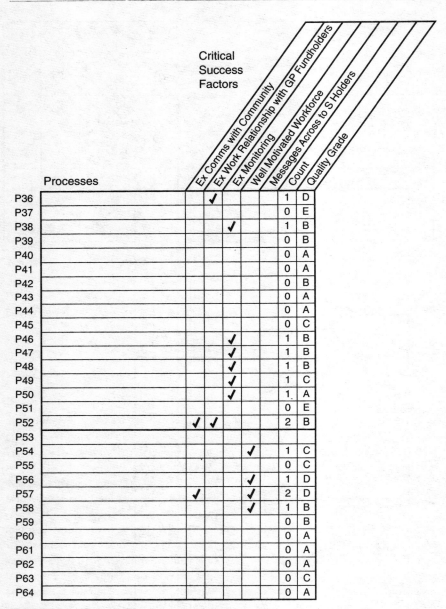

Processes	Ex Comms with Community	Ex Work Relationship with GP Fundholders	Ex Monitoring	Well Motivated Workforce	Messages Across to S Holders	Count	Quality Grade
P36	✓					1	D
P37						0	E
P38			✓			1	B
P39						0	B
P40						0	A
P41						0	A
P42						0	B
P43						0	A
P44						0	A
P45						0	C
P46			✓			1	B
P47			✓			1	B
P48			✓			1	B
P49			✓			1	C
P50			✓			1	A
P51						0	E
P52	✓	✓				2	B
P53							
P54				✓		1	C
P55						0	C
P56				✓		1	D
P57	✓			✓		2	D
P58				✓		1	B
P59						0	B
P60						0	A
P61						0	A
P62						0	A
P63						0	C
P64						0	A

Figure 17.3 (Continued).

		A	B	C	D	E
Orientating the Players	25	0	2	2	3	5
Developing the Market	16	5	4	4	1	0
Managing the Market	7	3	2	4	2	2
Monitoring the Market	7	3	5	2	0	1
Developing and Managing the Health Authority	5	4	2	3	2	0

Figure 17.4 *Quality rating of processes.*

people to be referred to providers with whom the Health Authority has no established contract.

The request for an extra contractual referral (ECR) is usually made by a general practitioner. The GP is required to describe the patient's requirements in order that the contracting department can make a judgement as to whether a contract is available for the condition with an established provider.

The system is open to manipulation by both GPs and their patients.

ECRs are usually high cost, for complex treatment and/or for new techniques which may be of unproved value. Additionally, because there is no nationally agreed criterion for giving certain treatments (for example, the treatment of infertile couples) patients may ask their GP to refer them to a centre which they know will accept them.

In cases of female infertility, for example, some centres will not accept women aged over 40, in others there may be a higher age limit; some centres will give three treatments; some will give six.

Each year as part of the budget-setting process the Health Authority earmarks a sum of money for ECRs. There is no way of knowing at the beginning of the financial year how many or what type of requests for ECRs the authority will receive. It is not unusual for the ECR budget to be topped two or three times during the year using financial reserves from other sources. If the Authority was unable to find extra monies for ECRs the implication would be very adverse media attention!

In the last financial year, Dumplington spent £2.5 million on ECRs. This equates to £50,000 per week with an average value of £10,000, or an average of five successful ECRs every week.

Process

Requests are either received in writing from GPs, or a telephone request is made to the ECR manager who is part of the contracts department. Details are entered onto a computerised database.

The ECR manager then checks to see whether a current contract covers the treatment requested. The ECR manager then asks the Director of Public Health for an opinion on the clinical aspects of the case.

The Director of Public Health formulates a judgement by discussing the proposed treatment with the provider unit clinicians and then by accessing health literature on the procedure from the textual database within the organisation.

If there are no sound clinical grounds for the request, for example the treatment is of doubtful clinical value, then the Director of Public Health contacts the referring GP to explain why the request is being refused. There is no consistency in respect of following up this conversation in writing.

If there is good clinical evidence for the request and a centre who will provide the service can be identified, the ECR manager then sets up a contract with that provider. The GP is asked to make the referral as s/he would normally do.

The provider receives written confirmation of the contractual agreement which will cover the procedure to be performed, the cost and the process for requesting payment. These details are entered onto the database in the contracting department.

The patient receives their treatment and the provider submits the bill for the treatment to the ECR manager.

The ECR manager then checks the bill against the agreed contract and, if appropriate, authorises the bill for payment and passes it to the finance department for payment.

The finance clerk checks the ECR budget and makes the payment if there is still money in the ECR budget. The finance clerk inputs the information regarding the request into the finance database using the information which the ECR manager has provided.

If no money is available the finance clerk reports the matter to the Associate Director responsible for contract monitoring. The Associate Director then reports the matter to the Director of Finance who reports on the ECR position to the management team.

A decision is then taken at team level about whether to transfer money across and from where this will come.

The Finance Director instructs the Associate Director to transfer the funds and adjust the budget. The Associate Director, in turn, instructs the finance clerk.

The finance clerk transfers the funds, adjusts the budget and the payment is made.

The management team provides reports to the Health Authority members at each of their meetings. The report provides information on the cost and volume of ECRs. At the end of the financial year the Executive Director responsible for contracting analyses the ECR position to identify whether routine contracts need to be established with providers of some of the treatments.

It is more advantageous to do this because ECR prices tend to be a higher cost than prices for procedures where a guaranteed level of referrals can be made. Where this happens negotiations are then undertaken by the contracting team.

Whilst ECR management has been identified as a separate process with lead responsibility falling to the Director of Contracting, this process has clear links with other processes as follows: 1, 2, 8, 9, 11, 12, 22, 28, 29, 39, 46, 48, 51.

The process flowchart shown in Figure 17.5 details what is happening in the process.

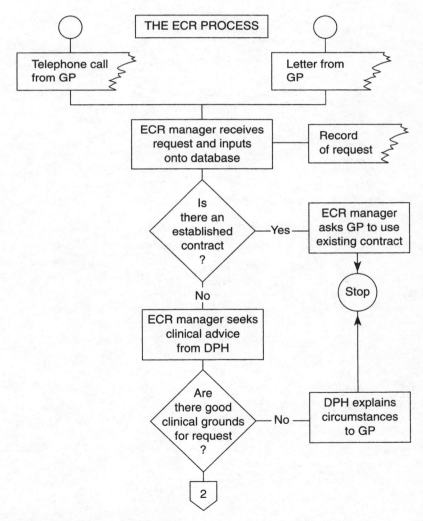

Figure 17.5 *The ECR process flowchart.*

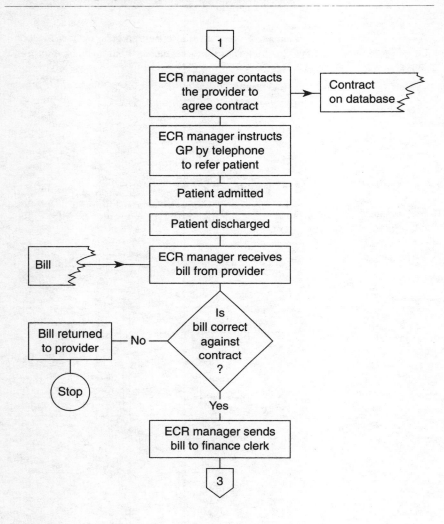

Figure 17.5 *(Continued).*

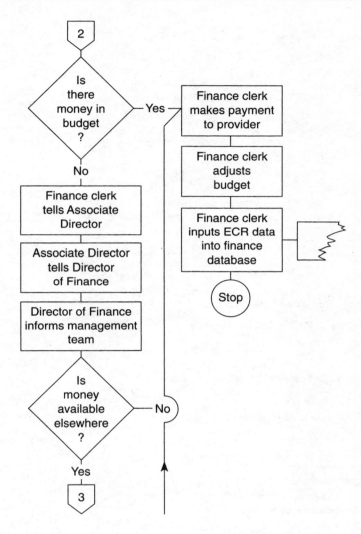

Figure 17.5 *(Continued).*

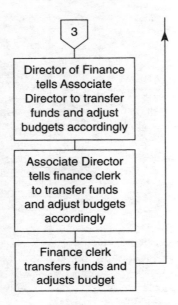

Figure 17.5 *(Continued).*

External partners for this process are:

▦ GPs/GP fundholders;
▦ Community Health Council;
▦ the public.

The key customers of this process are:

▦ *Internal:*
  – chairman and members;
  – executive directors;
  – finance staff.
▦ *External:*
  – GPs;
  – members of the public;
  – provider units.

Key outputs of the process are:

▦ a clear audit trail and analysis of ECRs;
▦ approval of ECRs in line with DHA policy and financial constraints.

Key objectives of the process are:

▦ To hold the volume and cost of ECRs at the lowest possible level by means of effective control and by identifying situations where contractual arrangements should be developed.

Options for Improvement

An improvement team was set up to examine the process in detail and look for ways to speed up the process and reduce or remove budget overspends.

The Re-engineering Option

At one level, the team realised that this process should not exist at all, since it was usually possible for the GPs to take the decision without reference to the Director of Public Health.

Therefore if business process re-engineering was the approach to be followed one possible solution would have been to provide GPs with terminals with access to the database used by the Director of Public Health. This would remove the process from the Health Authority and place it where it belonged, effectively changing the boundaries between the general practitioners and the Health Authority.

In the event a decision was taken that it would be politically very difficult to do this and that the adverse publicity would be damaging.

The Process Simplification Option

As a budget control process the process as described is clearly very inefficient since the money has been spent before the budget checks are done.

The process was not acting as designed as a budget control process so the improvement team agreed a change to move the authorisation of the surgical procedure to after the cash availability had been checked. This change resulted in far fewer overspends and budget changes.

Although there were other problems with the process the team decided at that stage to work on the new process to examine the effectiveness.

Analysis of the Process

Examination of the ECR flowchart in Figure 17.5 shows that there are two items of importance:

- the length of time taken to process the ECR request;
- the number of rejected ECRs and the reasons for these.

The team began to collect data on the timeliness of the request by date stamping the request on input and again on output and then subtracting the two dates to find the length of time taken to process the ECR.

As explained earlier, an average of five ECRs are successfully processed each week together with a number of unsuccessful requests.

Data was collected over an the month of September and the ECRs followed until completion, as follows:

Extra contractual referral data

No.	Date requested	Date resolved	No. of days
1	4/9/95	12/9/95	7
2	4/9/95	25/9/95	16
3	5/9/95	11/9/95	5
4	5/9/95	12/9/95	6
5	6/9/95	13/9/95	6
6	6/9/95	28/9/95	17
7	7/9/95	13/9/95	5
8	11/9/95	18/9/95	6
9	11/9/95	18/9/95	6
10	12/9/95	4/10/95	17
11	13/9/95	19/9/95	5
12	14/9/95	22/9/95	7
13	15/9/95	6/10/95	16
14	15/9/95	22/9/95	6
15	18/9/95	28/9/95	9
16	18/9/95	27/9/95	8
17	18/9/95	22/9/95	5
18	19/9/95	6/10/95	14
19	19/9/95	22/9/95	4
20	20/9/95	10/10/95	15
21	21/9/95	29/9/95	7
22	22/9/95	3/10/95	8
23	25/9/95	3/10/95	7
24	25/9/95	16/10/95	16
25	26/9/95	16/10/95	15
26	26/9/95	3/10/95	6
27	27/9/95	5/10/95	7
28	27/9/95	19/10/95	16
29	29/9/95	10/10/95	8
30	29/9/95	11/10/95	9

This data was transferred onto a tally chart to get a picture of any patterns in the time to complete an ECR, as follows:

Tally chart of ECR data

Days to process	Tally	Count
1	.	0
2	.	0
3	.	0
4	I	1
5	IIII	4
6	I ₶	6
7	₶	5
8	III	3
9	II	2
10	.	0
11	.	0
12	.	0
13	.	0
14	I	1
15	II	2
16	IIII	4
17	II	2
18	.	0
Total		30

From the tally chart a much clearer picture emerges of what is happening with the data.

A histogram can then be drawn using the same data, as shown in Figure 17.6.

Analysis of the situation revealed that the data is showing two distributions that are mixed together – the distribution of rejected requests and the distribution of accepted requests. The two peaks correspond to the centres of the two distributions.

This data could be taken a stage further by monitoring the situation using a control chart. In this case the correct type of chart would be the x moving range chart – the data is variable data and there is only one time reading taken.

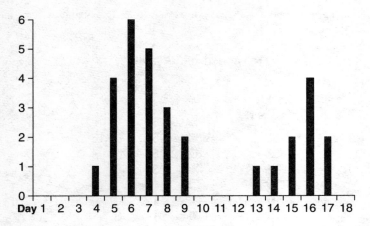

Figure 17.6 *Histogram of ECR data.*

The first step is to construct the moving range as follows:

Extra contractual referral data

No.	Date requested	Date resolved	No. of days	Moving range
1	4/9/95	12/9/95	7	
2	4/9/95	25/9/95	16	9
3	5/9/95	11/9/95	5	11
4	5/9/95	12/9/95	6	1
5	6/9/95	13/9/95	6	0
6	6/9/95	28/9/95	17	11
7	7/9/95	13/9/95	5	12
8	11/9/95	18/9/95	6	1
9	11/9/95	18/9/95	6	0
10	12/9/95	4/10/95	17	11
11	13/9/95	19/9/95	5	12
12	14/9/95	22/9/95	7	2
13	15/9/95	6/10/95	16	9
14	15/9/95	22/9/95	6	10
15	18/9/95	28/9/95	9	3
16	18/9/95	27/9/95	8	1
17	18/9/95	22/9/95	5	3
18	19/9/95	6/10/95	14	9
19	19/9/95	22/9/95	4	10

20	20/9/95	10/10/95	15	11
21	21/9/95	29/9/95	7	8
22	22/9/95	3/10/95	8	1
23	25/9/95	3/10/95	7	1
24	25/9/95	16/10/95	16	9
25	26/9/95	16/10/95	15	1
26	26/9/95	3/10/95	6	9
27	27/9/95	5/10/95	7	1
28	27/9/95	19/10/95	16	9
29	29/9/95	10/10/95	8	8
30	29/9/95	11/10/95	9	1

The sum of the times and the sum of the moving ranges are then calculated and the average values found. Remember that whilst there are 30 time values there are only 29 moving ranges.

Extra contractual referral data

No.	Date requested	Date resolved days	No. of range	Moving
1	4/9/95	12/9/95	7	
2	4/9/95	25/9/95	16	9
3	5/9/95	11/9/95	5	11
4	5/9/95	12/9/95	6	1
5	6/9/95	13/9/95	6	0
6	6/9/95	28/9/95	17	11
7	7/9/95	13/9/95	5	12
8	11/9/95	18/9/95	6	1
9	11/9/95	18/9/95	6	0
10	12/9/95	4/10/95	17	11
11	13/9/95	19/9/95	5	12
12	14/9/95	22/9/95	7	2
13	15/9/95	6/10/95	16	9
14	15/9/95	22/9/95	6	10
15	18/9/95	28/9/95	9	3
16	18/9/95	27/9/95	8	1
17	18/9/95	22/9/95	5	3
18	19/9/95	6/10/95	14	9
19	19/9/95	22/9/95	4	10
20	20/9/95	10/10/95	15	11
21	21/9/95	29/9/95	7	8
22	22/9/95	3/10/95	8	1
23	25/9/95	3/10/95	7	1

24	25/9/95	16/10/95	16	9
25	26/9/95	16/10/95	15	1
26	26/9/95	3/10/95	6	9
27	27/9/95	5/10/95	7	1
28	27/9/95	19/10/95	16	9
29	29/9/95	10/10/95	8	8
30	29/9/95	11/10/95	9	1
Sum			342	174
Mean			11.4	6.0

So the two centre lines are:

$$\bar{x} = \Sigma x/30 = 11.4$$
$$\bar{R} = \Sigma R/29 = 6.0$$

The control lines for the x chart can now be calculated as:

$$\begin{aligned} \text{UCL}_x &= \bar{x} + \bar{R}/d_2 \\ &= 11.4 + 6.0/1.128 \\ &= 11.4 + 5.3 \\ &= 16.7 \end{aligned}$$

and:

$$\begin{aligned} \text{LCL}_x &= \bar{x} - \bar{R}/d_2 \\ &= 11.4 - 5.3 \\ &= 6.1 \end{aligned}$$

So the x chart is as in Figure 17.7.

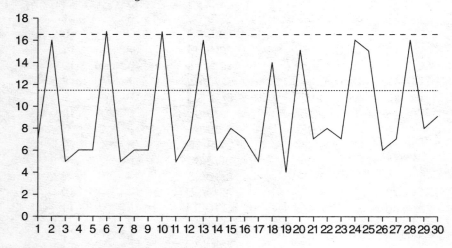

Figure 17.7 *The x chart for the ECR data.*

The control lines for the R chart are:

$$\begin{aligned} UCL_R &= D_4 \times \overline{R} \\ &= 3.27 \times 6.0 \\ &= 19.2 \end{aligned}$$

and:

$$\begin{aligned} LCL_R &= D_3 \times \overline{R} \\ &= 0 \times 6 \\ &= 0 \end{aligned}$$

The R chart then appears as in Figure 17.8.

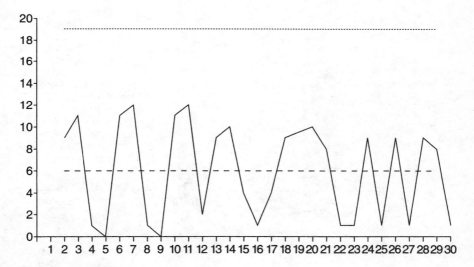

Figure 17.8 *The R chart for the ECR data.*

Examination firstly of the R chart reveals that the situation is in control. Next, examination of the x chart shows that the process is out of statistical control with points above and below the control lines.

This is a reflection of the fact that there are in fact two processes mixed together – the process for handling the accepted ECRs and the second process for those that are rejected.

An improvement team was set up to collect data on the causes of rejection of the ECRs and to look for ways of eradicating the problem. The data collected over a three-month period showed the following pattern:

Reason for rejection	Count
Treatment already available	89
Non-proven efficacy	13
Too costly	8

Using this data a Pareto chart was calculated:

Reason for rejection	Count	%	Cum. %
Treatment already available	89	89	89
Non-proven efficacy	13	13	92
Too costly	8	8	100
Total	100		

The Pareto chart in Figure 17.9 shows this in pictorial form.

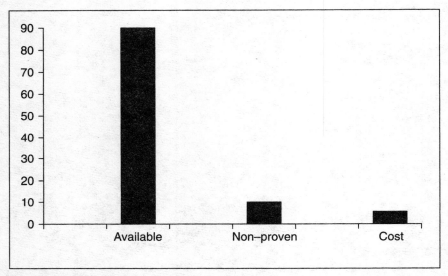

Figure 17.9 *Pareto chart for reasons for deferral.*

The team then looked into reasons why patients were being referred for treatments that already existed.

They first of all brainstormed the possible causes and then placed them on a cause and effect diagram as shown in Figure 17.10.

Further investigation and data collection revealed that the actual cause was the lack of up-to-date information in the hands of the GPs. When this problem was remedied the number of referrals dropped sharply.

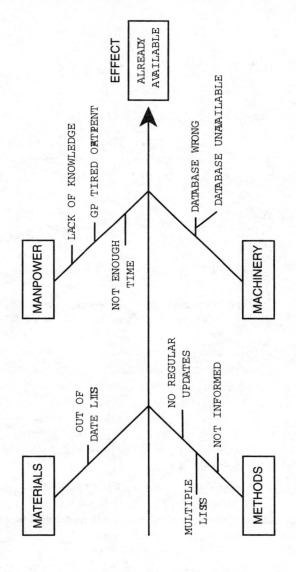

Figure 17.10 *Cause and effect diagram for causes of treatment being already available.*

APPENDIX 1

DEFINITIONS

Attribute A *characteristic* that is appraised in terms of whether it meets or does not meet a given requirement (eg go/no go, good/bad, pass/fail).

Capability A measure of the ability of a process to produce to the specified requirement; it relates the spread of a process to the specified requirement.

Characteristic A particular property of an item. Sometimes called an *element* or a *feature*.

Common disturbance A source of variation affecting all values which is consistent and predictable.

Control chart A chart with *control limits* on which are plotted values of *variables* or *attributes* for a series of *samples*. The chart frequently shows a central *mean* line to assist detection of patterns in the plotted values.

Control limits Limits on a *control chart* that are used to indicate when a process is out of statistical control.

Defective An item that fails to comply with its specified requirements.

Distribution A way of describing the output from a process in terms of its pattern or shape.

Frequency A curve representing the form to which the *distribution curve* frequency distribution tends as more and more observations are gathered.

Histogram A graphical means of presenting information where frequency of observation is arranged in order of observed size.

Mean An arithmetic average: the sum of observations divided by the number of observations.

Normal A distribution used in the theory of *control distribution charts*. It is depicted graphically by a symmetrical bell-shaped or normal frequency distribution curve.

Pareto analysis
A graphical means of presenting information where groups of similar data are arranged in order of magnitude. Its purpose is to show where to start taking action.

Population
The total quantity of items that are under consideration.

Process
The combination of people, machines, materials, methods and environment that produces a given product or service.

Process control
The gathering of data from a process, the use of control charts and other statistical techniques and the establishment of feedback loops to achieve and maintain a state of statistical control.

Process variability
The degree of variability which exists in a process that is in statistical control.

Proportion or fraction defective
The number of defective items divided by the total number of items inspected. Multiplied by 100, the fraction defective gives the 'per cent defective'.

Range
The difference between the maximum and minimum observations in a sample.

Sample
A single item or group of items taken randomly from a *population*. It provides information on a *characteristic* (or characteristics) to assess the need and responsibility for action on the process that produced it.

Special disturbance
A source of variation that is intermittent, unpredictable, unstable; sometimes called an assignable or special cause. It is signalled usually by a point on a *control chart* beyond the *control limits* or a non-random pattern of points within the control limits.

Standard deviation
A measure of the spread or dispersion of a distribution, equal to the square root of the average of the squares of all individual deviations from the mean in the *sample*.

Statistical control
A stable state that allows prediction of variation in the characteristics of the products of a process. Also, the absence of *special disturbances*.

Variable
A *characteristic* that is appraised in terms of values on a continuous scale.

APPENDIX 2

STATISTICAL SYMBOLS

x	Value of variable
$\bar{x}$	The average of a set of values or mean
s	Standard deviation of a sample
n	The number of units (sample size)
m	The number of samples taken
R	Range from highest to lowest value
$\bar{R}$	Mean of several sample ranges
$\bar{\bar{x}}$	$\bar{x}$ mean of several $\bar{x}$ values
P	Proportion of non-conforming units in a sample
$\bar{p}$	Average proportion of non-conforming units in a series of samples (weighted by sample size)
np	Number of non-conforming items in a constant sample size
$\overline{np}$	Average number of non-conforming items in samples of constant size
c	Number of non-conformities (defects) in a sample
$\bar{c}$	Average number of non-conformities in samples of constant size
u	Number of non-conformities per unit in a sample which may contain more than one unit
$\bar{u}$	Average number of non-conformities per unit in samples not necessarily of the same size
C_p	A capability index, a measure of the spread of the process in terms of the specified limits
UCL	Upper control limit of a control chart
LCL	Lower control limit of a control chart
USL	Upper specified limit
LSL	Lower specified limit
$\sqrt{}$	The square root of

APPENDIX 3
TABLE OF CONSTANTS

n	2	3	4	5	6	7	8	9	10
A_2	1.88	1.02	0.73	0.58	0.48	0.42	0.37	0.34	0.31
D_3	0	0	0	0	0	0.08	0.14	0.18	0.22
D_4	3.27	2.57	2.28	2.11	2.00	1.92	1.86	1.82	1.78
d_2	1.13	1.69	2.06	2.33	2.53	2.70	2.85	2.97	3.08

APPENDIX 4
STANDARDISED TAILS OF PEARSON
CURVES (POSITIVE SKEWNESS)

Skewness (Sk) — *... percentile of Sk < 0.*

Ku	2.0	1.9	1.8	1.7	1.6	1.5	1.4	1.3	1.2	1.1	1.0	0.9	0.8	0.7	0.6	0.5	0.4	0.3	0.2	0.1	0.0	Ku
-1.4														0.762	0.868	0.979	1.092	1.206	1.317	1.421	1.512	-1.4
-1.2													0.747	0.858	0.975	1.100	1.230	1.364	1.496	1.619	1.727	-1.2
-1.0											0.692	0.804	0.836	0.957	1.089	1.232	1.384	1.541	1.696	1.840	1.966	-1.0
-0.8											0.766	0.887	0.927	1.062	1.212	1.377	1.555	1.736	1.912	2.072	2.210	-0.8
-0.6										0.658	0.841	0.974	1.023	1.175	1.348	1.539	1.740	1.941	2.129	2.298	2.442	-0.6
-0.4									0.616	0.723	0.933	1.063	1.125	1.299	1.496	1.711	1.930	2.141	2.335	2.506	2.653	-0.4
-0.2								0.574	0.677	0.789	1.008	1.159	1.235	1.434	1.655	1.887	2.116	2.329	2.522	2.692	2.839	-0.2
0.0							0.531	0.630	0.739	0.861	1.086	1.269	1.355	1.578	1.821	2.053	2.289	2.500	2.689	2.856	3.000	0.0
0.2							0.583	0.686	0.801	0.933	1.175	1.382	1.485	1.726	1.976	2.229	2.449	2.653	2.834	2.986	3.140	0.2
0.4						0.536	0.635	0.742	0.865	1.008	1.277	1.502	1.619	1.873	2.127	2.368	2.589	2.785	2.952	3.088	3.261	0.4
0.6					0.489	0.583	0.685	0.799	0.931	1.087	1.381	1.625	1.754	2.015	2.267	2.502	2.714	2.896	3.045	3.164	3.366	0.6
0.8					0.533	0.629	0.736	0.857	1.000	1.172	1.491	1.748	1.887	2.148	2.396	2.622	2.821	2.986	3.115	3.222	3.458	0.8
1.0				0.489	0.575	0.675	0.787	0.917	1.072	1.262	1.602	1.876	2.013	2.271	2.512	2.727	2.910	3.058	3.174	3.266	3.539	1.0
1.2				0.524	0.617	0.721	0.840	0.979	1.149	1.357	1.713	1.981	2.132	2.385	2.616	2.817	2.983	3.115	3.218	3.300	3.611	1.2
1.4			0.475	0.562	0.659	0.768	0.894	1.045	1.230	1.456	1.821	2.089	2.243	2.488	2.708	2.893	3.043	3.161	3.254	3.327	3.674	1.4
1.6		0.461	0.510	0.600	0.701	0.815	0.950	1.113	1.316	1.556	1.925	2.189	2.345	2.581	2.787	2.957	3.092	3.199	3.282	3.349	3.731	1.6
1.8	0.445	0.494	0.546	0.638	0.743	0.863	1.008	1.185	1.404	1.664	2.023	2.283	2.438	2.664	2.855	3.011	3.133	3.229	3.306	3.367	3.782	1.8
2.0	0.475	0.526	0.580	0.676	0.785	0.913	1.068	1.261	1.494	1.755	2.116	2.369	2.524	2.736	2.914	3.055	3.167	3.255	3.325	3.382	3.828	2.0
2.2	0.504	0.557	0.615	0.714	0.828	0.964	1.132	1.339	1.584	1.850	2.202	2.448	2.600	2.800	2.964	3.093	3.196	3.277	3.342	3.395	3.870	2.2
2.4	0.533	0.589	0.649	0.752	0.873	1.018	1.198	1.420	1.673	1.940	2.283	2.521	2.669	2.855	3.006	3.126	3.220	3.295	3.356	3.405	3.908	2.4
2.6	0.562	0.620	0.683	0.791	0.918	1.073	1.267	1.501	1.760	2.026	2.358	2.586	2.730	2.904	3.043	3.153	3.241	3.311	3.367	3.415	3.943	2.6
2.8	0.590	0.651	0.717	0.830	0.965	1.131	1.338	1.581	1.844	2.107	2.427	2.646	2.784	2.946	3.075	3.177	3.259	3.324	3.378	3.423	3.975	2.8
3.0	0.618	0.681	0.752	0.870	1.013	1.191	1.410	1.661	1.924	2.183	2.491	2.699	2.831	2.983	3.103	3.198	3.274	3.336	3.387	3.430	4.004	3.0
3.2	0.646	0.712	0.787	0.911	1.063	1.253	1.483	1.738	2.000	2.254	2.549	2.747	2.874	3.015	3.127	3.216	3.288	3.346	3.395	3.436	4.031	3.2
3.4	0.674	0.742	0.822	0.953	1.115	1.317	1.555	1.813	2.072	2.321	2.602	2.790	2.911	3.043	3.149	3.233	3.300	3.356	3.402	3.441	4.056	3.4
3.6	0.702	0.775	0.858	0.996	1.169	1.381	1.626	1.884	2.140	2.383	2.651	2.829	2.945	3.069	3.168	3.247	3.311	3.364	3.408	3.446	4.079	3.6
3.8	0.730	0.807	0.895	1.040	1.224	1.446	1.695	1.953	2.205	2.440	2.695	2.864	2.974	3.091	3.184	3.259	3.321	3.371	3.414	3.450	4.101	3.8
4.0	0.758	0.839	0.932	1.088	1.284	1.510	1.762	2.018	2.266	2.494	2.735	2.895	3.000	3.111	3.199	3.271	3.329	3.377	3.419	3.454	4.121	4.0
4.2	0.786	0.872	0.971	1.134	1.346	1.574	1.827	2.080	2.324	2.544	2.775	2.923	3.025	3.129	3.213	3.281	3.336	3.384	3.423	3.458	4.140	4.2
4.4	0.815	0.905	1.011	1.184	1.398	1.636	1.889	2.138	2.374	2.588	2.805	2.949	3.047	3.145	3.225	3.290	3.344	3.389	3.428	3.461	4.157	4.4
4.6	0.844	0.939	1.052	1.234	1.453	1.697	1.948	2.194	2.424	2.629	2.835	2.972	3.066	3.160	3.236	3.299	3.350	3.394	3.431	3.464	4.174	4.6
4.8	0.874	0.975	1.094	1.285	1.510	1.756	2.005	2.246	2.470	2.668	2.863	2.994	3.084	3.173	3.246	3.306	3.356	3.399	3.435	3.466	4.189	4.8
5.0	0.904	1.010	1.137	1.336	1.566	1.813	2.059	2.296	2.513	2.703	2.888	3.013	3.100	3.186	3.256	3.313	3.362	3.403	3.438	3.469	4.204	5.0
5.2	0.935	1.047	1.181	1.387	1.621	1.867	2.111	2.342	2.553	2.735	2.911	3.031	3.114	3.197	3.264	3.320	3.367	3.406	3.441	3.471	4.218	5.2
5.4	0.966	1.085	1.225	1.438	1.675	1.920	2.160	2.386	2.589	2.765	2.933	3.047	3.128	3.207	3.272	3.326	3.371	3.410	3.444	3.473	4.231	5.4
5.6	0.999	1.123	1.270	1.489	1.727	1.970	2.206	2.427	2.624	2.793	2.952	3.062	3.140	3.216	3.279	3.331	3.375	3.413	3.446	3.475	4.243	5.6
5.8	1.031	1.162	1.316	1.539	1.778	2.019	2.250	2.465	2.656	2.818	2.967	3.076	3.152	3.225	3.286	3.336	3.379	3.416	3.449	3.477	4.255	5.8
6.0	1.065	1.202	1.361	1.588	1.827	2.065	2.292	2.501	2.685	2.841	2.982	3.089	3.162	3.233	3.292	3.341	3.383	3.419	3.451	3.478	4.266	6.0
6.2	1.099	1.242	1.407	1.635	1.874	2.109	2.332	2.535	2.713	2.863	3.003	3.100	3.172	3.240	3.297	3.345	3.386	3.421	3.453	3.481	4.276	6.2
6.4	1.134	1.282	1.452	1.682	1.919	2.151	2.369	2.567	2.739	2.883	3.017	3.111	3.181	3.247	3.303	3.349	3.389	3.424	3.456	3.483	4.286	6.4
6.6	1.169	1.323	1.496	1.727	1.962	2.191	2.405	2.597	2.763	2.902	3.030	3.122	3.189	3.254	3.308	3.353	3.392	3.426	3.458	3.484	4.296	6.6
6.8	1.204	1.363	1.540	1.771	2.004	2.229	2.438	2.624	2.785	2.919	3.043	3.131	3.197	3.260	3.312	3.357	3.395	3.429	3.459	3.485	4.305	6.8
7.0	1.240	1.403	1.583	1.814	2.044	2.265	2.469	2.651	2.806	2.936	3.054	3.140	3.204	3.265	3.316	3.360	3.398	3.431	3.461	3.486	4.313	7.0
7.2	1.276	1.443	1.625	1.855	2.083	2.300	2.499	2.675	2.825	2.951	3.065	3.148	3.211	3.270	3.321	3.363	3.400	3.432	3.463	3.487	4.322	7.2
7.4	1.311	1.482	1.666	1.895	2.120	2.333	2.527	2.698	2.843	2.965	3.075	3.156	3.218	3.275	3.324	3.366	3.403	3.434	3.464	3.489	4.330	7.4
7.6	1.347	1.521	1.706	1.933	2.155	2.364	2.554	2.720	2.860	2.978	3.085	3.164	3.224	3.280	3.328	3.369	3.405	3.436	3.466	3.490	4.337	7.6
7.8	1.382	1.559	1.744	1.971	2.189	2.394	2.579	2.740	2.876	2.990	3.095	3.171	3.229	3.284	3.331	3.372	3.407	3.438	3.467	3.491	4.344	7.8
8.0	1.418	1.596	1.782	2.007	2.222	2.422	2.603	2.760	2.890	3.002	3.104	3.177	3.235	3.289	3.334	3.374	3.409	3.439	3.468	3.492	4.351	8.0
8.2	1.452	1.632	1.818	2.045	2.252	2.449	2.625	2.777	2.906	3.012	3.111	3.183	3.240	3.292	3.338	3.377	3.411	3.441	3.469	3.493	4.358	8.2
8.4	1.486	1.667	1.854	2.070	2.282	2.475	2.646	2.794	2.919	3.023	3.118	3.189	3.244	3.296	3.340	3.379	3.413	3.443	3.470	3.494	4.365	8.4
8.6	1.520	1.702	1.888	2.104	2.310	2.499	2.666	2.810	2.932	3.033	3.125	3.195	3.249	3.300	3.343	3.381	3.414	3.444	3.471	3.495	4.371	8.6
8.8	1.553	1.736	1.921	2.135	2.337	2.522	2.685	2.825	2.943	3.042	3.132	3.200	3.253	3.303	3.345	3.383	3.416	3.445	3.472	3.495	4.377	8.8
9.0	1.586	1.769	1.953	2.164	2.363	2.544	2.703	2.839	2.955	3.051	3.138	3.205	3.257	3.306	3.348	3.385	3.417	3.446	3.473	3.495	4.382	9.0
9.2	1.617	1.800	1.984	2.192	2.388	2.565	2.720	2.852	2.965	3.059	3.144	3.209	3.261	3.309	3.351	3.387	3.419	3.448	3.474	3.496	4.388	9.2
9.4	1.648	1.831	2.014	2.219	2.411	2.585	2.736	2.866	2.975	3.067	3.150	3.214	3.265	3.312	3.353	3.388	3.420	3.449	3.474	3.496	4.393	9.4
9.6	1.679	1.861	2.042	2.245	2.434	2.604	2.752	2.878	2.985	3.075	3.156	3.218	3.268	3.315	3.355	3.390	3.421	3.449	3.475	3.497	4.398	9.6
9.8	1.708	1.890	2.070	2.271	2.456	2.622	2.766	2.890	2.994	3.082	3.161	3.222	3.272	3.317	3.357	3.392	3.422	3.450			4.403	9.8
10.0	1.737	1.918	2.097	2.295	2.476	2.639	2.780	2.901	3.003	3.088	3.166	3.226	3.275	3.320	3.359	3.393	3.423	3.451			4.408	10.0
10.2	1.765	1.945	2.123	2.318	2.496	2.655	2.793	2.911	3.011	3.095	3.171	3.230	3.278	3.322	3.361	3.395						10.2
10.4	1.793	1.972	2.148	2.340	2.515	2.671	2.806	2.921	3.019	3.101	3.175	3.233	3.281	3.325	3.363	3.396						10.4
10.6	1.819	1.998	2.172	2.361	2.533	2.686	2.818	2.930	3.026	3.107	3.179	3.237	3.283									10.6
10.8	1.845	2.023	2.196	2.382	2.551	2.700	2.829	2.940	3.033	3.112	3.184	3.240	3.286									10.8
11.0	1.870	2.047	2.218	2.401	2.567	2.714	2.840	2.948	3.040	3.118	3.188	3.243	3.289									11.0
11.2	1.895	2.070	2.240	2.420	2.583	2.727	2.851	2.956	3.046	3.123	3.191											11.2
11.4	1.919	2.093	2.261	2.438	2.598	2.739	2.861	2.964	3.053	3.128	3.195											11.4
11.6	1.942	2.115	2.281	2.456	2.613	2.751	2.870	2.972	3.058	3.132												11.6
11.8	1.965	2.136	2.301	2.473	2.627	2.762	2.879	2.979	3.064													11.8
12.0		2.157	2.320	2.489	2.641	2.773	2.888	2.986	3.070													12.0
12.2			2.338	2.505	2.653	2.784	2.896	2.993	3.075													12.2
Sk ->	2.0	1.9	1.8	1.7	1.6	1.5	1.4	1.3	1.2	1.1	1.0	0.9	0.8	0.7	0.6	0.5	0.4	0.3	0.2	0.1	0.0	

APPENDIX 5
STANDARDISED TAILS OF PEARSON
CURVES (NEGATIVE SKEWENESS)

Appendix 5 ■ 207

Up' (99.865 percentile) for Sk >= 0, Lp' (0.135 percentile) for Sk < 0.

Skewness (Sk)

Kurtosis Ku	0.0	0.1	0.2	0.3	0.4	0.5	0.6	0.7	0.8	0.9	1.0	1.1	1.2	1.3	1.4	1.5	1.6	1.7	1.8	1.9	2.0	Ku
-1.4	1.512	1.584	1.632	1.655	1.653	1.626	1.579	1.516														-1.4
-1.2	1.727	1.813	1.871	1.899	1.895	1.861	1.803	1.726	1.636													-1.2
-1.0	1.966	2.065	2.134	2.170	2.169	2.131	2.061	1.966	1.856	1.822												-1.0
-0.8	2.210	2.320	2.400	2.446	2.454	2.422	2.349	2.241	2.108	2.052	1.965											-0.8
-0.6	2.442	2.560	2.648	2.704	2.726	2.708	2.646	2.540	2.395	2.314	2.225	1.885										-0.6
-0.4	2.653	2.774	2.869	2.934	2.969	2.968	2.926	2.837	2.699	2.608	2.518	2.114	1.928									-0.4
-0.2	2.839	2.961	3.060	3.133	3.179	3.194	3.173	3.109	2.993	2.914	2.824	2.373	2.152	1.952								-0.2
0.0	3.000	3.123	3.224	3.303	3.358	3.387	3.385	3.345	3.259	3.206	3.116	2.665	2.412	2.169	1.960							0.0
0.2	3.140	3.261	3.364	3.447	3.510	3.550	3.564	3.546	3.488	3.468	3.378	2.970	2.690	2.412	2.167	2.149						0.2
0.4	3.261	3.381	3.484	3.570	3.639	3.688	3.715	3.715	3.681	3.693	3.603	3.264	2.984	2.687	2.398	2.366	2.119					0.4
0.6	3.366	3.485	3.588	3.676	3.749	3.805	3.843	3.858	3.844	3.883	3.793	3.529	3.283	2.984	2.658	2.609	2.322	2.269				0.6
0.8	3.458	3.575	3.678	3.768	3.844	3.905	3.951	3.978	3.981	4.043	3.953	3.758	3.561	3.283	2.945	2.881	2.547	2.476	2.399			0.8
1.0	3.539	3.654	3.757	3.847	3.926	3.991	4.044	4.080	4.096	4.177	4.087	3.952	3.781	3.581	3.243	3.178	2.798	2.706	2.609	2.511		1.0
1.2	3.611	3.724	3.826	3.917	3.997	4.066	4.124	4.167	4.194	4.290	4.298	4.120	3.998	3.808	3.529	3.472	3.076	2.961	2.840	2.719	2.603	1.2
1.4	3.674	3.786	3.887	3.979	4.060	4.131	4.195	4.243	4.278	4.386	4.376	4.311	4.200	4.015	3.729	3.729	3.365	3.238	3.095	2.949	2.808	1.4
1.6	3.731	3.842	3.942	4.033	4.115	4.189	4.253	4.308	4.351	4.468	4.449	4.479	4.372	4.209	4.015	3.974	3.646	3.522	3.370	3.201	3.033	1.6
1.8	3.782	3.891	3.990	4.081	4.164	4.239	4.307	4.365	4.414	4.539	4.511	4.549	4.521	4.381	4.209	4.189	3.907	3.796	3.648	3.471	3.280	1.8
2.0	3.828	3.936	4.034	4.125	4.208	4.285	4.354	4.416	4.468	4.600	4.564	4.620	4.627	4.521	4.372	4.369	4.137	4.047	3.916	3.745	3.544	2.0
2.2	3.870	3.976	4.073	4.164	4.248	4.325	4.396	4.460	4.517	4.653	4.611	4.682	4.693	4.627	4.510	4.521	4.336	4.269	4.160	4.007	3.813	2.2
2.4	3.908	4.013	4.109	4.199	4.283	4.361	4.433	4.500	4.559	4.700	4.653	4.736	4.758	4.678	4.627	4.649	4.506	4.460	4.376	4.247	4.072	2.4
2.6	3.943	4.046	4.142	4.231	4.315	4.394	4.467	4.535	4.597	4.741	4.700	4.783	4.812	4.756	4.725	4.758	4.650	4.623	4.563	4.461	4.311	2.6
2.8	3.975	4.077	4.172	4.261	4.344	4.423	4.498	4.567	4.631	4.777	4.741	4.824	4.860	4.824	4.809	4.850	4.771	4.762	4.723	4.647	4.524	2.8
3.0	4.004	4.105	4.199	4.287	4.371	4.450	4.525	4.596	4.662	4.810	4.777	4.861	4.903	4.882	4.881	4.929	4.875	4.880	4.859	4.806	4.712	3.0
3.2	4.031	4.131	4.224	4.312	4.396	4.475	4.550	4.622	4.689	4.839	4.810	4.893	4.940	4.932	4.944	4.996	4.946	4.980	4.976	4.943	4.873	3.2
3.4	4.056	4.155	4.247	4.335	4.418	4.498	4.573	4.645	4.714	4.865	4.839	4.922	4.973	4.976	4.997	5.055	5.038	5.066	5.075	5.059	5.012	3.4
3.6	4.079	4.177	4.269	4.356	4.439	4.518	4.594	4.667	4.737	4.888	4.865	4.948	5.002	5.015	5.049	5.106	5.103	5.139	5.159	5.159	5.131	3.6
3.8	4.101	4.197	4.288	4.375	4.458	4.537	4.614	4.687	4.757	4.910	4.888	4.972	5.029	5.049	5.085	5.150	5.159	5.202	5.232	5.244	5.233	3.8
4.0	4.121	4.217	4.307	4.393	4.476	4.555	4.631	4.705	4.776	4.929	4.910	4.993	5.054	5.080	5.122	5.189	5.208	5.257	5.295	5.318	5.320	4.0
4.2	4.140	4.234	4.324	4.410	4.492	4.571	4.648	4.722	4.794	4.947	4.929	5.012	5.074	5.107	5.153	5.223	5.250	5.305	5.349	5.381	5.395	4.2
4.4	4.157	4.251	4.340	4.425	4.508	4.587	4.663	4.737	4.809	4.963	4.947	5.029	5.093	5.131	5.181	5.253	5.288	5.346	5.396	5.436	5.460	4.4
4.6	4.174	4.267	4.355	4.440	4.522	4.601	4.677	4.752	4.824	4.978	4.963	5.045	5.109	5.152	5.207	5.280	5.321	5.383	5.437	5.483	5.516	4.6
4.8	4.189	4.281	4.369	4.454	4.535	4.614	4.691	4.765	4.838	4.992	4.978	5.060	5.126	5.172	5.229	5.303	5.350	5.415	5.474	5.523	5.565	4.8
5.0	4.204	4.295	4.383	4.467	4.548	4.627	4.703	4.778	4.851	5.004	4.992	5.073	5.141	5.190	5.249	5.325	5.376	5.443	5.504	5.561	5.608	5.0
5.2	4.218	4.308	4.395	4.479	4.560	4.638	4.715	4.789	4.862	5.016	5.004	5.085	5.154	5.206	5.267	5.346	5.396	5.468	5.533	5.593	5.645	5.2
5.4	4.231	4.321	4.407	4.490	4.571	4.649	4.725	4.800	4.873	5.025	5.016	5.096	5.164	5.222	5.284	5.361	5.418	5.491	5.558	5.621	5.678	5.4
5.6	4.243	4.332	4.418	4.501	4.581	4.659	4.735	4.810	4.884	5.037	5.025	5.106	5.177	5.233	5.299	5.380	5.436	5.511	5.581	5.646	5.708	5.6
5.8	4.255	4.343	4.428	4.511	4.591	4.669	4.745	4.820	4.893	5.046	5.037	5.116	5.188	5.257	5.312	5.390	5.452	5.529	5.600	5.669	5.734	5.8
6.0	4.266	4.354	4.439	4.521	4.600	4.676	4.754	4.829	4.902	5.055	5.046	5.125	5.197	5.276	5.325	5.404	5.467	5.542	5.618	5.688	5.758	6.0
6.2	4.276	4.364	4.448	4.530	4.609	4.687	4.763	4.837	4.911	5.063	5.055	5.134	5.206	5.293	5.336	5.414	5.480	5.557	5.634	5.706	5.775	6.2
6.4	4.286	4.373	4.457	4.538	4.618	4.695	4.771	4.845	4.919	5.071	5.063	5.143	5.214	5.308	5.346	5.425	5.492	5.569	5.648	5.722	5.792	6.4
6.6	4.296	4.382	4.466	4.547	4.626	4.703	4.778	4.853	4.926	5.078	5.071	5.150	5.222	5.320	5.356	5.434	5.503	5.581	5.658	5.736	5.808	6.6
6.8	4.305	4.391	4.474	4.554	4.633	4.710	4.785	4.860	4.933	5.084	5.078	5.157	5.229	5.331	5.364	5.443	5.513	5.591	5.669	5.749	5.823	6.8
7.0	4.313	4.399	4.481	4.562	4.640	4.717	4.792	4.867	4.940	5.090	5.084	5.164	5.236	5.341	5.372	5.451	5.522	5.601	5.679	5.760	5.836	7.0
7.2	4.322	4.406	4.489	4.569	4.647	4.724	4.799	4.873	4.946	5.095	5.091	5.170	5.242	5.349	5.380	5.459	5.530	5.609	5.688	5.771	5.847	7.2
7.4	4.330	4.414	4.496	4.576	4.654	4.730	4.805	4.879	4.952	5.098	5.097	5.175	5.248	5.357	5.387	5.466	5.538	5.617	5.696	5.779	5.859	7.4
7.6	4.337	4.421	4.503	4.582	4.660	4.736	4.811	4.885	4.958		5.109	5.181	5.253	5.364	5.393	5.472	5.545	5.624	5.704	5.790	5.867	7.6
7.8	4.344	4.428	4.509	4.588	4.666	4.742	4.817	4.890	4.963		5.114	5.186	5.259	5.367	5.404	5.478	5.551	5.631	5.710	5.797	5.875	7.8
8.0	4.351	4.434	4.515	4.594	4.672	4.747	4.822	4.896	4.969		5.118	5.191	5.263	5.370	5.414	5.483	5.557	5.637	5.717	5.803	5.883	8.0
8.2	4.358	4.441	4.521	4.600	4.677	4.753	4.827	4.901	4.974		5.123	5.195	5.268	5.373	5.423	5.488	5.562	5.642	5.722	5.808	5.889	8.2
8.4	4.365	4.447	4.527	4.605	4.682	4.758	4.832	4.905	4.978		5.127	5.200	5.272	5.375	5.427	5.493	5.567	5.647	5.727	5.813	5.894	8.4
8.6	4.371	4.452	4.532	4.611	4.687	4.762	4.837	4.910	4.983		5.132	5.204	5.276	5.378	5.431	5.497	5.572	5.652	5.732	5.817	5.898	8.6
8.8	4.377	4.458	4.538	4.616	4.692	4.767	4.841	4.914	4.987		5.135	5.208	5.280	5.380	5.437	5.501	5.576	5.656	5.736	5.821	5.903	8.8
9.0	4.382	4.463	4.543	4.621	4.697	4.772	4.845	4.918	4.991		5.139	5.211	5.284	5.383	5.440	5.505	5.580	5.660	5.740	5.825	5.906	9.0
9.2	4.388	4.468	4.548	4.625	4.701	4.776	4.850	4.923	4.995		5.143	5.214	5.287	5.385	5.443	5.509	5.584	5.663	5.744	5.828	5.910	9.2
9.4	4.393	4.473	4.552	4.630	4.705	4.780	4.854	4.927	5.002		5.146	5.218	5.291	5.389	5.446	5.513	5.588	5.667	5.747	5.831	5.913	9.4
9.6	4.398	4.478	4.557	4.634	4.710	4.784	4.857	4.930	5.006		5.150	5.222	5.294	5.391	5.451	5.515	5.591	5.670	5.750	5.834	5.915	9.6
9.8	4.403	4.483	4.561	4.638	4.714	4.788	4.861	4.934	5.009		5.153	5.225	5.297	5.393	5.454	5.518	5.593	5.673	5.753	5.836	5.918	9.8
10.0	4.408	4.487	4.565	4.642	4.717	4.791	4.865	4.937	5.012		5.156	5.228	5.300	5.394	5.456	5.521	5.596	5.675	5.755	5.838	5.920	10.0
10.2	4.408	4.487			4.721	4.795	4.868	4.940	5.015		5.158	5.230	5.303		5.458	5.523	5.599	5.678	5.757	5.840	5.922	10.2
10.4						4.798	4.871	4.943	5.018		5.161	5.233	5.305		5.460	5.526	5.601	5.680	5.760	5.842	5.924	10.4
10.6							4.874	4.947	5.021		5.164	5.236	5.308		5.462	5.528	5.603	5.682	5.762	5.844	5.925	10.6
10.8								4.949	5.024		5.166	5.238	5.310		5.464	5.530	5.605	5.684	5.763	5.845	5.927	10.8
11.0											5.169	5.240	5.312		5.465	5.532	5.607	5.686	5.765	5.847	5.928	11.0
11.2											5.171	5.243	5.314		5.467	5.534	5.609	5.687	5.767	5.848		11.2
11.4											5.173	5.245	5.316			5.536	5.611	5.689	5.768			11.4
11.6												5.247	5.318			5.538	5.613	5.690	5.769			11.6
11.8												5.249	5.320			5.539	5.614	5.692				11.8
12.0													5.322			5.541	5.616					12.0
12.2			4.565	4.642	4.721	4.798	4.874	4.949	5.024	5.098	5.173	5.249	5.322	5.394	5.467	5.541	5.616	5.692	5.769	5.848	5.928	12.2
Sk ->	0.0	0.1	0.2	0.3	0.4	0.5	0.6	0.7	0.8	0.9	1.0	1.1	1.2	1.3	1.4	1.5	1.6	1.7	1.8	1.9	2.0	

APPENDIX 6
STANDARDISED MEDIAN OF PEARSON CURVES

M' (50 percentile). Change sign for Sk >0

Kurtosis / Skewness (Sk)

Ku	0.0	0.1	0.2	0.3	0.4	0.5	0.6	0.7	0.8	0.9	1.0	1.1	1.2	1.3	1.4	1.5	1.6	1.7	1.8	1.9	2.0	Ku
–1.4	0.000	0.053	0.111	0.184	0.282	0.424	0.627	0.754														–1.4
–1.2	0.000	0.039	0.082	0.132	0.196	0.284	0.412	0.591	0.727													–1.2
–1.0	0.000	0.031	0.065	0.103	0.151	0.212	0.297	0.419	0.586													–1.0
–0.8	0.000	0.026	0.054	0.085	0.123	0.169	0.231	0.317	0.439	0.598	0.681											–0.8
–0.6	0.000	0.023	0.047	0.073	0.104	0.142	0.190	0.254	0.343	0.468	0.616	0.653										–0.6
–0.4	0.000	0.020	0.041	0.064	0.091	0.122	0.161	0.212	0.280	0.375	0.504	0.633	0.616									–0.4
–0.2	0.000	0.018	0.037	0.058	0.081	0.108	0.141	0.183	0.237	0.311	0.413	0.542	0.638	0.574								–0.2
0.0	0.000	0.017	0.034	0.053	0.073	0.097	0.126	0.161	0.206	0.266	0.347	0.456	0.578	0.621	0.531							0.0
0.2	0.000	0.015	0.032	0.049	0.068	0.089	0.114	0.145	0.183	0.233	0.299	0.388	0.501	0.605	0.582							0.2
0.4	0.000	0.014	0.029	0.045	0.063	0.082	0.105	0.132	0.165	0.208	0.263	0.336	0.433	0.545	0.607	0.536						0.4
0.6	0.000	0.013	0.028	0.043	0.059	0.077	0.097	0.122	0.151	0.188	0.235	0.297	0.379	0.481	0.579	0.579	0.489					0.6
0.8	0.000	0.013	0.026	0.040	0.055	0.072	0.091	0.113	0.140	0.172	0.213	0.266	0.336	0.425	0.527	0.590	0.533					0.8
1.0	0.000	0.012	0.025	0.038	0.053	0.068	0.086	0.106	0.130	0.159	0.196	0.242	0.301	0.379	0.474	0.563	0.569	0.484				1.0
1.2	0.000	0.011	0.024	0.036	0.050	0.065	0.082	0.100	0.122	0.148	0.181	0.222	0.274	0.341	0.426	0.520	0.576	0.524				1.2
1.4	0.000	0.011	0.023	0.035	0.048	0.062	0.078	0.095	0.116	0.140	0.169	0.206	0.252	0.310	0.385	0.474	0.554	0.555	0.475			1.4
1.6	0.000	0.010	0.022	0.034	0.046	0.060	0.074	0.091	0.110	0.132	0.159	0.192	0.233	0.285	0.351	0.432	0.518	0.564	0.510			1.6
1.8	0.000	0.010	0.021	0.032	0.044	0.057	0.072	0.087	0.105	0.126	0.151	0.180	0.217	0.264	0.323	0.396	0.480	0.549	0.540	0.461		1.8
2.0	0.000	0.009	0.020	0.031	0.043	0.055	0.069	0.084	0.101	0.120	0.143	0.171	0.204	0.246	0.299	0.365	0.443	0.521	0.552	0.494		2.0
2.2	0.000	0.009	0.020	0.030	0.042	0.054	0.067	0.081	0.097	0.115	0.137	0.162	0.193	0.231	0.279	0.338	0.410	0.488	0.544	0.522	0.445	2.2
2.4	0.000	0.009	0.019	0.029	0.040	0.052	0.065	0.078	0.094	0.111	0.131	0.155	0.183	0.218	0.261	0.315	0.381	0.456	0.524	0.538	0.475	2.4
2.6	0.000	0.008	0.018	0.029	0.039	0.051	0.063	0.076	0.091	0.107	0.126	0.148	0.175	0.207	0.246	0.295	0.355	0.426	0.498	0.539	0.503	2.6
2.8	0.000	0.008	0.018	0.028	0.038	0.049	0.061	0.074	0.088	0.104	0.122	0.143	0.167	0.197	0.233	0.278	0.333	0.398	0.470	0.526	0.522	2.8
3.0	0.000	0.008	0.017	0.027	0.037	0.048	0.059	0.072	0.085	0.101	0.118	0.138	0.161	0.189	0.222	0.263	0.313	0.374	0.443	0.506	0.530	3.0
3.2	0.000	0.008	0.017	0.027	0.037	0.047	0.058	0.070	0.083	0.098	0.114	0.133	0.155	0.181	0.212	0.250	0.296	0.352	0.417	0.483	0.525	3.2
3.4	0.000	0.008	0.017	0.026	0.036	0.046	0.057	0.068	0.081	0.095	0.111	0.129	0.150	0.174	0.203	0.239	0.281	0.333	0.394	0.460	0.513	3.4
3.6	0.000	0.007	0.016	0.025	0.035	0.045	0.056	0.067	0.079	0.093	0.108	0.125	0.145	0.168	0.196	0.228	0.268	0.316	0.373	0.437	0.495	3.6
3.8	0.000	0.007	0.016	0.025	0.034	0.044	0.054	0.066	0.078	0.091	0.105	0.122	0.141	0.163	0.188	0.219	0.256	0.301	0.354	0.415	0.475	3.8
4.0	0.000	0.007	0.015	0.025	0.034	0.043	0.053	0.064	0.076	0.089	0.103	0.119	0.137	0.158	0.182	0.211	0.246	0.288	0.337	0.395	0.455	4.0
4.2	0.000	0.007	0.015	0.024	0.033	0.043	0.053	0.063	0.075	0.087	0.101	0.116	0.133	0.153	0.176	0.204	0.236	0.276	0.322	0.376	0.435	4.2
4.4	0.000	0.007	0.015	0.024	0.033	0.042	0.052	0.062	0.073	0.085	0.099	0.113	0.130	0.149	0.171	0.197	0.228	0.265	0.308	0.359	0.416	4.4
4.6	0.000	0.007	0.015	0.023	0.032	0.041	0.051	0.061	0.072	0.084	0.097	0.111	0.127	0.145	0.167	0.191	0.220	0.255	0.296	0.344	0.399	4.6
4.8	0.000	0.006	0.015	0.023	0.032	0.041	0.050	0.060	0.071	0.082	0.095	0.109	0.124	0.142	0.162	0.186	0.213	0.246	0.285	0.330	0.382	4.8
5.0	0.000	0.006	0.014	0.023	0.031	0.040	0.049	0.059	0.070	0.081	0.093	0.107	0.122	0.139	0.158	0.181	0.207	0.238	0.274	0.317	0.367	5.0
5.2	0.000	0.006	0.014	0.022	0.031	0.040	0.049	0.058	0.069	0.080	0.092	0.105	0.119	0.138	0.155	0.176	0.201	0.231	0.265	0.306	0.353	5.2
5.4	0.000	0.006	0.014	0.022	0.030	0.039	0.048	0.057	0.068	0.078	0.090	0.103	0.117	0.133	0.151	0.172	0.196	0.224	0.257	0.295	0.340	5.4
5.6	0.000	0.006	0.014	0.022	0.030	0.039	0.047	0.057	0.067	0.077	0.089	0.101	0.115	0.131	0.148	0.168	0.191	0.218	0.249	0.285	0.328	5.6
5.8	0.000	0.006	0.014	0.022	0.030	0.038	0.047	0.056	0.066	0.076	0.087	0.100	0.113	0.128	0.145	0.164	0.186	0.212	0.242	0.277	0.317	5.8
6.0	0.000	0.006	0.014	0.021	0.029	0.038	0.046	0.055	0.065	0.075	0.086	0.098	0.111	0.126	0.142	0.161	0.182	0.207	0.235	0.268	0.307	6.0
6.2	0.000	0.006	0.013	0.021	0.029	0.037	0.046	0.055	0.064	0.074	0.085	0.097	0.110	0.124	0.140	0.158	0.178	0.202	0.229	0.261	0.298	6.2
6.4	0.000	0.006	0.013	0.021	0.029	0.037	0.045	0.054	0.063	0.073	0.084	0.096	0.108	0.122	0.137	0.155	0.175	0.197	0.223	0.254	0.289	6.4
6.6	0.000	0.006	0.013	0.021	0.028	0.037	0.045	0.054	0.063	0.073	0.083	0.094	0.107	0.120	0.135	0.152	0.171	0.193	0.218	0.247	0.281	6.6
6.8	0.000	0.006	0.013	0.021	0.028	0.036	0.044	0.053	0.062	0.072	0.082	0.093	0.105	0.118	0.133	0.150	0.168	0.189	0.213	0.241	0.273	6.8
7.0	0.000	0.005	0.013	0.020	0.028	0.036	0.044	0.053	0.061	0.071	0.081	0.092	0.104	0.117	0.131	0.147	0.165	0.185	0.209	0.236	0.267	7.0
7.2	0.000	0.005	0.013	0.020	0.028	0.036	0.044	0.052	0.061	0.070	0.080	0.091	0.103	0.115	0.129	0.145	0.162	0.182	0.205	0.230	0.260	7.2
7.4	0.000	0.005	0.013	0.020	0.027	0.035	0.043	0.052	0.060	0.070	0.079	0.090	0.101	0.114	0.128	0.143	0.160	0.179	0.201	0.226	0.254	7.4
7.6	0.000	0.005	0.012	0.020	0.027	0.035	0.043	0.051	0.060	0.069	0.079	0.089	0.100	0.113	0.126	0.141	0.157	0.176	0.197	0.221	0.249	7.6
7.8	0.000	0.005	0.012	0.020	0.027	0.035	0.043	0.051	0.059	0.068	0.078	0.088	0.099	0.111	0.124	0.139	0.155	0.173	0.193	0.217	0.243	7.8
8.0	0.000	0.005	0.012	0.019	0.027	0.034	0.042	0.050	0.059	0.068	0.077	0.087	0.098	0.110	0.123	0.137	0.153	0.170	0.190	0.213	0.238	8.0
8.2	0.000	0.005	0.012	0.019	0.027	0.034	0.042	0.050	0.058	0.067	0.076	0.086	0.097	0.109	0.121	0.135	0.151	0.168	0.187	0.209	0.234	8.2
8.4	0.000	0.005	0.012	0.019	0.026	0.034	0.042	0.050	0.058	0.067	0.076	0.086	0.096	0.108	0.120	0.134	0.149	0.165	0.184	0.205	0.229	8.4
8.6	0.000	0.005	0.012	0.019	0.026	0.034	0.041	0.049	0.057	0.066	0.075	0.085	0.095	0.107	0.119	0.132	0.147	0.163	0.181	0.202	0.225	8.6
8.8	0.000	0.005	0.012	0.019	0.026	0.033	0.041	0.049	0.057	0.066	0.075	0.084	0.094	0.106	0.118	0.131	0.145	0.161	0.179	0.199	0.221	8.8
9.0	0.000	0.005	0.012	0.019	0.026	0.033	0.041	0.049	0.057	0.065	0.074	0.084	0.094	0.105	0.116	0.129	0.143	0.159	0.176	0.196	0.218	9.0
9.2	0.000	0.005	0.012	0.019	0.026	0.033	0.040	0.048	0.056	0.065	0.073	0.083	0.093	0.104	0.115	0.128	0.142	0.157	0.174	0.193	0.214	9.2
9.4	0.000	0.005	0.012	0.019	0.026	0.033	0.040	0.048	0.056	0.064	0.073	0.082	0.092	0.103	0.114	0.127	0.140	0.155	0.172	0.190	0.211	9.4
9.6	0.000	0.005	0.012	0.019	0.025	0.033	0.040	0.048	0.055	0.064	0.072	0.082	0.091	0.102	0.113	0.125	0.139	0.153	0.170	0.188	0.208	9.6
9.8	0.000	0.005	0.012	0.018	0.025	0.032	0.040	0.047	0.055	0.063	0.072	0.081	0.091	0.101	0.112	0.124	0.137	0.152	0.168	0.185	0.205	9.8
10.0	0.000	0.005	0.011	0.018	0.025	0.032	0.040	0.047	0.055	0.063	0.071	0.080	0.090	0.100	0.111	0.123	0.136	0.150	0.166	0.183	0.202	10.0
10.2	0.000					0.032	0.039	0.047	0.054	0.063	0.071	0.080	0.089	0.099	0.110	0.122	0.135	0.149	0.164	0.181	0.200	10.2
10.4	0.000					0.032	0.039	0.047	0.054	0.062	0.071	0.079	0.089	0.099	0.109	0.121	0.133	0.147	0.162	0.179	0.197	10.4
10.6	0.000						0.039	0.046	0.054	0.062	0.070	0.079	0.088	0.098	0.109	0.120	0.132	0.146	0.160	0.177	0.195	10.6
10.8	0.000							0.046	0.054	0.061	0.070	0.078	0.088	0.097	0.108	0.119	0.131	0.144	0.159	0.175	0.192	10.8
11.0	0.000								0.053	0.061	0.069	0.078	0.087	0.097	0.107	0.118	0.130	0.143	0.157	0.173	0.190	11.0
11.2	0.000									0.061	0.069	0.078	0.087	0.096	0.106	0.117	0.129	0.142	0.156	0.171	0.188	11.2
11.4	0.000										0.069	0.077	0.086	0.095	0.105	0.116	0.128	0.141	0.154	0.169	0.186	11.4
11.6	0.000										0.068	0.077	0.086	0.095	0.104	0.116	0.127	0.139	0.153	0.168	0.184	11.6
11.8	0.000											0.076	0.085	0.094	0.104	0.115	0.126	0.138	0.152	0.166	0.182	11.8
12.0	0.000											0.076	0.085	0.094	0.104	0.114	0.125	0.137	0.150	0.165	0.181	12.0
12.2	0.000												0.084	0.093	0.103	0.113	0.124	0.136	0.149	0.163	0.179	12.2
Sk ->	0.0	0.1	0.2	0.3	0.4	0.5	0.6	0.7	0.8	0.9	1.0	1.1	1.2	1.3	1.4	1.5	1.6	1.7	1.8	1.9	2.0	

APPENDIX 7
CALCULATION WORKSHEETS

The worksheets in this section give calculations for all of the different methods of monitoring process performance and calculating process capability. The author waives any copyright on these and encourages readers to copy them and use them freely.

x̄ – R CONTROL CHART FOR MEAN AND RANGE

Control Limits

Sub-groups included m =

Sub-group size n =

Sum of R ΣR =

Sum of $\bar{x}$ $\Sigma \bar{x}$ =

CL $\bar{\bar{x}} = \Sigma\bar{x}/m$ =

CL $\bar{R} = \Sigma R/m$ =

$UCL_R = D_4 \times \bar{R}$ =

$LCL_R = D_3 \times \bar{R}$ =

$A_2 \times \bar{R}$ =

$UCL_{\bar{x}} = \bar{\bar{x}} + A_2 \times \bar{R}$ =

$LCL_{\bar{x}} = \bar{\bar{x}} - A_2 \times \bar{R}$ =

Factors for Control Limits

n	A_2	d_4	D_3
2	1.88	3.27	0
3	1.02	2.57	0
4	0.73	2.28	0
5	0.58	2.11	0
6	0.48	2.00	0

Out of Control Conditions

	R	x
Points out		
Shifts		
Trends		

Comments

P CONTROL CHART FOR FRACTION DEFECTIVE

Control Limits

Sub-groups included m =

Total sub-group size Σn =

Total defects Σnp =

$\bar{n} = \Sigma n / m$ =

$\bar{p} = \Sigma np / \Sigma n$ =

Centre line $\bar{p}$ % $= \bar{p} \times 100$ =

$3 \times \sqrt{\bar{p}}$ =

$\sqrt{(1 - \bar{p})}$ =

$k = 3 \times \sqrt{\bar{p}} \times \sqrt{(1 - \bar{p}}$ =

$UCL_p = \bar{p} + k/\sqrt{\bar{n}}$ =

$LCL_p = \bar{p} - k/\sqrt{\bar{n}}$ =

$UCL_p\% = UCL_p \times 100\%$ =

$LCL_p\% = LCL_p \times 100\%$ =

Out of Control Conditions

Points out

Shifts

Trends

Comments

U CONTROL CHART FOR FRACTION DEFECTS

Control Limits

Sub-groups included m =

Total sub-group size Σn =

Total defects Σc =

$\bar{n} = \Sigma n/m$ =

$\bar{u} = \Sigma c/\Sigma n$ =

Centre line $\bar{u}$ % $= \bar{u} \times 100$ =

$k = 3 \times \sqrt{\bar{u}}$ =

$UCL_u = \bar{u} + k/\sqrt{\bar{n}}$ =

$LCL_u = \bar{u} - k/\sqrt{\bar{n}} =$

$UCL_u\% = UCL_u \times 100\%$ =

$LCL_u\% = LCL_u \times 100\%$ =

Out of Control Conditions

Points out

Shifts

Trends

Comments

PROCESS CAPABILITY WORKSHEET

$\bar{\bar{x}}$ =

$\bar{R}$ =

Upper specification limit USL =

Lower specification limit LSL =

$\hat{S} = \bar{R}/d_2$ =

$C_{pk} = (\bar{\bar{x}} - LSL)/3\hat{S}$=

or

$C_{pk} = (USL - \bar{\bar{x}})/3\hat{S}$=

whichever is the smaller

Factors for Capability

n	d_2
2	1.13
3	1.69
4	2.06
5	2.33
6	2.53

Comments

PROCESS CAPABILITY WORKSHEET
FOR NON-NORMAL DATA

Upper target value $\qquad$ U_t =

Process mean value $\qquad$ x =

Standard deviation $\qquad$ S =

Coefficient of skewness $\qquad$ C_s =

Coefficient of kurtosis $\qquad$ C_k =

Standardised 99.865 percentile from tables: $\quad U_p$ =
for positive skewness use Appendix 4
for negative skewness use Appendix 5

Standardised median from Appendix 6: $\qquad M_p$ =
for positive skewness reverse sign
for negative skewness leave positive

Calculate the estimated 99.865 percentile $\quad U_I$ = $\quad x + U_p\, S$

=

=

Calculate the estimated median $\qquad M$ = $\quad x + S \times M_p$

=

=

Capability index for upper tail $\qquad C_{pk}$ = $\dfrac{(U - M)}{(U_1 - M)}$

=

=

REFERENCES

Asher, J. M. (1991) 'Mission into Action', *Total Quality Management*, Vol. 2, No. 2 p. 119.

Born, G. (1994) *Process Management to Quality Improvement*. Wiley, New York.

Camp, R. C. (1989) *Benchmarking – The Search for Industry Best Practices that Lead to Superior Performance*. ASQC Industry Press, Milwaukee, Wisconsin.

Chang, R. and Niedzwiecki, M. (1993). *Continuous Improvement Tools*. Richard Chang, Irvine, California.

Clements, J. A. (1989) 'Process capability calculations for non-normal distributions', *Quality Progress*, September, p. 95.

Dale, B. G. and Plunkett, J. J. (1991) *Quality Costing*. Chapman & Hall, London.

Hammer, M. and Champy, J. (1993) *Re-engineering the Corporation*. Nicholas Brealey, London.

Hardaker, M. and Ward, B. K. (1987) 'Getting things done', *Harvard Business Review*, November/December, pp. 112–17.

Kane, V. E. (1989) *Defect Prevention*. Marcel Dekker, New York.

Kanji, G. K. and Asher, J. M. (1996) *100 Methods for Total Quality Management*. Sage, London.

Kume, H. (1995) *Statistical Methods for Quality Improvement*. AOTS, Tokyo.

Owen, M. (1989) *SPC and Business Improvement*. IFS Publications, London.

White Paper (1991) *Competing for Quality, Buying Better Public Services*. HMSO, London.

INDEX

References in *italic* indicate figures or tables.